W. Drott

THE TEN COMMANDMENTS
A Study of Ethical Freedom

THE TEN COMMANDMENTS

A Study of Ethical Freedom

RONALD S. WALLACE

Wm. B. Eerdmans Publishing Company
Grand Rapids, Michigan

Published in Great Britain by
Oliver & Boyd Ltd, Edinburgh and London

First Published 1965

PRINTED IN GREAT BRITAIN BY
HAZELL WATSON AND VINEY LTD
AYLESBURY, BUCKS

To T. F. Torrance

FOREWORD

I HAD originally intended to write a book containing no more than ten sermons, one on each Commandment. But as I faced the task it became obvious that I first had to undertake a preliminary study of the Biblical themes that are basic to an understanding of what the Commandments say. It then seemed that a more useful contribution could be made to the subject if I cast the results of this study into a readable form so that others who were also concerned about the interpretation of the Commandments could have this, rather than my own attempts at preaching, before them. This book is therefore simply a help to such basic Biblical study. Since it is written in the limited context of a preaching ministry, it will be understandable that the form which the study takes is sometimes homiletic, and that often the intention is to clarify an issue for those who have the task of preaching before them.

In the task of interpretation I have kept in mind the resolution Paul made when he went to Corinth: "I determined not to know anything among you, save Jesus Christ, and him crucified" (1 Cor. II.1). When I tried to preach on the Ten Commandments early in my ministry I found myself, under the guidance of most of the books I could then consult, speaking a good deal about principles, values, ideals, and virtues, and speaking also at times on the assumption that the Commandments were a summary of some kind of natural law written already in the consciences of those to whom I was speaking. My task, therefore, seemed to be little more than that of awakening men up to realise the importance of something they already knew, or should have known, quite apart from Jesus Christ.

I found myself soon dissatisfied and uneasy with this approach. My aim, in the treatment of other Biblical texts, had always been to expound them in the light of Jesus Christ alone. It now seemed strange that when I took my congregation to the heart of many of the moral problems they had to face in life, I should be failing to point directly in His direction.

Therefore I came to the conclusion that I must try to ignore those aspects of our traditional approach to the Commandments which involve the presuppositions of natural law and idealism, and try to interpret the Law by the Gospel, seeing each Commandment in the light of the whole Biblical message, and remembering that the central fact, to which both Old and New Testament witness, is the life, death, and resurrection of Jesus. Whether I have succeeded in producing a result consistent with the aim, the reader can judge. It is a very difficult matter to bring one's natural bent to natural theology into subjection to Jesus Christ. I have felt that a faithful exegesis of the first five Commandments must inevitably lead to an evangelical exposition of them, and this necessity dictates the way of approach to the understanding of the other five.

In my work for this book, I have read quite a number of standard works on Biblical ethics. I think I have learned how to approach ethical problems from Calvin and Barth. My debt to Barth, especially in the discussion of the fourth, sixth and seventh commandments will be obvious, even in the use of phraseology. I have read many books dealing directly with the Ten Commandments, e.g., by Dale, Dykes, Jackson, Quin, Luthi, Herklots, Charles, and Joy Davidman. Amongst these I found that Cosslett Quin's book gave me the most helpful clues, but I must acknowledge my debt to them all. I must also mention a helpful and unpublished paper by T. F. Torrance on the problem of the Sabbath, and my fellow members in the Scottish Church Theology Society whose wits have often sharpened mine, especially when we have discussed ethics, as we did at Crieff in 1962.

Is it justifiable to make the Ten Commandments the point at which we try to relate the Gospel to the important ethical questions of today? It is sometimes argued that this was not the practice in the early Church, and that, indeed, the Reformers themselves were mistaken in embodying the Ten Commandments so deeply in the discipline and tradition of Protestantism.

I would say, in reply, that as long as we seek seriously to listen to what the Old Testament as part of the whole Bible has to say to the Church, we are bound frequently to find that the Ten Commandments thrust themselves on our attention. They are one of the important focal points within the Bible. If they have been given prominence within the discipline of the Church, this is simply because they have prominence within the Word which the Church has sought to obey. There can be little doubt that at many points in the New Testament we are directly referred back to what they say. Even common sense will suggest the value of their use. They have the virtue of being short and memorable, and yet they are so comprehensive that their disciplined exegesis will force us to deal with every important ethical question, enabling us to avoid digression into matters that are secondary, and keeping each aspect of their challenge in its due proportion.

In writing this book, I have, of course, had to deal (as far as a parish minister can, who is not a specialist either in ethics or world affairs) with a number of the controversies raised by our present-day social, political, and theological problems. This all goes to confirm, again, how relevant the Ten Commandments are as a text for our preaching. But the exposition has not been directed primarily to answer these problems. The problems have, rather, been brought up for discussion at the points at which the exposition became relevant to them. The Word of God must be given priority even before our most acute problems.

I have to thank Mrs H. E. Cowper, a member of my congregation, for so kindly and carefully typing the MS.; my wife for her faithful criticisms and corrections of the MS. and the proofs; and the publishers for their unfailing help and courtesy.

Edinburgh   R. S. W.
February 1964

CONTENTS

Foreword   vii

Introduction: THE GLORIOUS LIBERTY OF THE CHILDREN OF GOD

  1. The good news at the heart of the Law   I

  2. The freedom of the people of God, and
     the grace which lies behind it   3

  3. The direction of the life of liberty   5

  4. The personal word for the concrete situation   7

  5. The call to self-denial   10

  6. The relevance of the whole Gospel for the
     whole of life   11

  7. "A light to the Gentiles"   12

THE FIRST COMMANDMENT

Chapter I: THE ULTIMATE CHOICE

  1. A strange and dangerous possibility   17

  2. The significance and power of the idol   17

  3. The gods around us to-day   19

  4. The exposure of the sham   21

  5. Command and promise   23

  6. A call to faith   26

THE SECOND COMMANDMENT

Chapter II: THE IMAGE OF THE INVISIBLE GOD

  1. The importance of words in the service of God   29

  2. The importance of images in the service of God   30

  3. The only true image of the invisible God   33

  4. The service of the image by Word and Sacrament   33

  5. The question of obedience   36

Chapter III: THE JEALOUSY THAT GUARDS GOD'S IMAGE

  1. An imageless God?   37

  2. A people in tension and conflict   39

3. God's strange jealousy 41

4. The mercy that lies behind God's jealousy 42

5. The conflict in the presence of Jesus 44

6. The continuing conflict today 46

THE THIRD COMMANDMENT

Chapter IV: THE FREEDOM TO WORSHIP AND PRAY

1. God gives Himself a name 51

2. The promises given with the name
   (i) The taking of oaths 53
   (ii) The invocation of God's presence 55

3. The warnings given with the name 57

4. Our abuse and neglect of the name 59

5. The challenge to our faith 61

THE FOURTH COMMANDMENT

Chapter V: THE MEANING OF THE SABBATH

1. God and His Sabbath 65

2. Man and the Sabbath 66

3. Christ and the Sabbath 71

Chapter VI: THE KEEPING OF THE SABBATH

1. The gift of the Sabbath 74

2. The keeping of the Sabbath by the Jew 74

3. The keeping of the Lord's day by the Christian Church 77

4. The universalising and legalising of the Sabbath by Church and State 81

5. The preservation of the Sabbath 82

THE FIFTH COMMANDMENT

Chapter VII: THE FREEDOM TO BUILD

1. The promise
   (i) God's long-term policy in the midst of history 85
   (ii) The aspects of the promise that are still in force 85

2. Inheriting the promise
    (i) The faith that Israel invested in the
         historical task   87
    (ii) Our mood of unsettlement   89
    (iii) The challenge "to build and to plant"   91
    (iv) The sober realism of faith   92

Chapter VIII: THE FREEDOM TO INHERIT

    1. The service of the promise by tradition and family   95

    2. The handing on of the promise by the passing
       generation   97

    3. The receiving of the promise by the rising
       generation   99

    4. The illumination of family life by the promise   102

    5. The illumination of the promise by family life   104

THE SIXTH COMMANDMENT

Chapter IX: THE FREEDOM TO LIVE

    1. The cosmic goal and significance of
       the redeeming work of God   107

    2. The promise of life for all   108

    3. The murderous world   109

    4. A call to continual repentance   111

    5. The protection of life   114

    6. Claiming the promise   116

THE SEVENTH COMMANDMENT

Chapter X: THE IMAGE OF GOD IN MARRIED LOVE

    1. The Gospel of Christ and the meaning of marriage   119

    2. The healing and restoration of the marriage
       relationship by Jesus Christ   122

    3. The essential implications of a marriage

        (i) Gift   124
        (ii) Task   125
        (iii) Covenant   129
        (iv) Fact   130

    4. The further implications of the task   132

Chapter XI: MARRIAGE, CHURCH, AND SOCIETY

1. An adulterous generation   134

2. A new pattern and new possibilities   138

3. The relevance of the pattern for Church,
   Society, and the individual   140

4. The acceptance of the pattern by Church,
   Society, and the individual   143

THE EIGHTH COMMANDMENT

Chapter XII: THE FREEDOM TO SHARE

1. The claim   151

2. The importance of the claim   151

3. The background against which the claim is made   152

4. The witness of the true Israel   155

5. The new order within the old   158

THE NINTH COMMANDMENT

Chapter XIII: THE FREEDOM OF THE TRUTH

1. The power of the lie   161

2. The things that are at stake when truth
   is at stake   162

3. The final eclipse and triumph of truth   165

4. Where our repentance must begin   167

5. The power of true witness in the service of Christ   169

THE TENTH COMMANDMENT

Chapter XIV: THE FREEDOM OF THE HEART

1. The heart of God's demand   173

2. The heart of the human problem   175

3. The heart of the cure   179

THE GLORIOUS LIBERTY OF THE CHILDREN OF GOD

EXODUS xx. 1–4. *And God spake all these words, saying, I am the Lord thy God, which have brought thee out of the land of Egypt, out of the house of bondage, Thou shalt. . . . Thou shalt not. . . .*

1. The good news at the heart of the Law

THE Ten Commandments have often been interpreted as if they were the summary of a rigid legal code demanding the strictest compliance with every letter, under the threat of dire penalty for failure to comply, laying on those who hear and understand, a heavy burden of new responsibility. The full and crushing nature of this burden, it is asserted, is revealed in the words of Jesus in the Sermon on the Mount about the inward meaning of the "Law," where He shows us that even hatred is murder, and even the lustful thought is adultery. With all this before us as the content of the Law we are meant to be driven to despair of ever being able to keep it, and thus forced to seek salvation, new birth, and help in Christ. The emphasis in such an interpretation lies on the imperatives, on the "shalt" or on the "shalt not," on the fact that the Commandments were given to Israel under awesome circumstance, accompanied by fire and earthquake, and also on the assumption that they were uttered with an accent unrelievedly terrifying.

The Commandments have also been interpreted as if they confronted us simply with something natural. It is suggested that when He gave them, God was outlining the moral constitution of His universe, and laying down basic natural rules which must be observed by men in every community if life is to be tolerable or if they are to survive. Such rules are supposed also to be written in the conscience of every man, and are given here in order to stimulate it to function properly. Under this view, a well-kept Sabbath day, for example, is regarded as such a necessary aspect of the life of a good and prosperous community that all men, whether they believe in God or not, must be compelled to keep it. The Ten Commandments on this assumption are simply the natural laws of ordinary life, on which all civil law should be based. They say nothing special. They hardly need to be argued for, or interpreted. Their essential meaning can be understood by the heathen as well as by the Christian.

Both these approaches to the interpretation of the Ten Commandments arise, certainly, from something that is within them. The Commandments, especially as inwardly interpreted by Jesus, can make us realise how much we need God's help even to begin to live as we ought. Certainly, too, the purpose for which God was redeeming Israel was in order that they might begin to live what might be described as a good and natural life.

But both interpretations miss the main truth, and emphasise as the central theme something that is, and should always remain, secondary. When we prepare ourselves to listen to what the Commandments are saying to us, instead of allowing the accompanying thunder to come to the foreground in the sound picture, we must tune it into the background, and concentrate on the tone of the voice and the actual content of the Word spoken. Then we find that we are confronted by what is gracious rather than terrifying, by something far too wonderful to be regarded only as natural, by the offer of love rather than the imposition of a rigid and burdensome code, by a promise more than by a demand. What must be seen in the background, as we look afresh at the Ten Commandments, is not the thunder and lightning on Sinai, but the wonderful redeeming fact of love, that brought God down into the midst of His people to deliver them from their bondage, for He saw their sorrows.

This does not mean that we are to forget entirely the thunderings and visible threats that form the circumstantial background of the giving of the Commandments. It is a fearful thing to fall into the hands of such a loving and living God. Here is a grace that can be rejected only under peril of utter destruction. Here in this loving command is the only way to liberty and peace, and all other ways are impossible. The thunder indeed is so terrifying that it is all the more important that we should hear the good news at the heart of the Law.

2. The freedom of the people of God, and the grace which lies behind it

"I am the Lord thy God which have brought thee out of the land of Egypt, out of the house of bondage." These words reminded the Children of Israel of their freedom. Through hearing them constantly repeated, and through having to repeat them, each generation of the Children of Israel was meant to grow up understanding itself as having passed beyond the fate of bitter slavery into a destiny of glorious liberty. As a people redeemed by God, a great deliverance—of which the Exodus of their fathers from Egypt was simply a typical shadow—lay behind them, decisive, complete, and glorious. "Your bondage is over for ever," these Commandments said to them, "your enemies have been destroyed as completely as Pharaoh and his chariots and horsemen. No decision of yours can take you back or alter the utter completeness of what has been once-for-all done for you. You are free, because I have come near to you in your helplessness, and delivered you and yours decisively from the hands of all your enemies and from every future possibility of destruction."

But it was not only their liberty that was emphasised in the repetition of these words, it was also the sheer undeserved grace that lay behind their liberty. None of them, listening to the Commandments, could have escaped this emphasis, for their history had been the history of a naturally godless people with no instinct for true faith at all. The Old Testament story is the story of the shame, the suffering, the rejection, the dishonour that fell on the name of God when He said to this people, "I am the Lord your God, who have made you mine, and made you free in making you mine!" How quickly they always forgot Him, how easily they always deserted Him, how perversely they used the gift of freedom which He had given them, and how deliberately and gleefully they stoned His prophets! But always He stands beside them, faithful to this word, and to this irrevocable decision of almighty Love, made for them and their generations for ever: "I am the Lord your God."

The Commandments begin with this reminder of the grace that has liberated the people of God, because this grace has now to be the motive for all their conduct towards God and towards man. Now they are to learn to obey God out of overflowing gratitude for a deliverance free, undeserved, and irreversible. In their response to God's Word there must be not a shadow of fear that their ultimate salvation is to depend on the obedience which is now called forth from them. They have to learn to live not in the hope of attaining salvation by moral or religious striving, but in the sheer gladness of a salvation already freely given by a God who knows all their weakness, and is aware of all the havoc that their rebellious natures can work in His plans. The God who calls them to His service has already saved them decisively from all the consequences of their disobedience, has maintained His hold of them even though in their liberty they have turned against Him time and again, spitefully and stubbornly. He will hold on to them for ever, with a longsuffering and majesty that no amount of human sin can exhaust or modify.

It is remarkable that when we listen to the Ten Commandments today in the light of Christ and the teaching of the New Testament, this aspect of them applies as directly to us as it ever did to the men of Israel. If we believe in Jesus Christ and find our lives caught up into the worship and fellowship of the Church, we are bound to come more and more to understand that the story of God and Israel is the story of God and ourselves. It is the story of the sheer grace that has liberated us sinful men and women from a hopeless and empty fate. The New Testament constantly urges us to think of ourselves as those for whom the death and resurrection of Jesus was an exodus (Lk. ix. 31 Gk. N.T.) by which we too are "brought out" from the bondage of darkness, death and vanity, into the light and life and glorious liberty of the children of God, and the kingdom of God's dear son (Col. i. 13). This is why Christians, if they believe in Jesus, are described in the New

Testament as those who are "dead," "crucified," "buried," "raised," "ascended," in and with Jesus and because of what | Jesus has done. Included in His once-for-all sacrifice and victory, united to Him by faith, and sharing in His love they are "dead indeed unto sin but alive unto God" (Rom. VI.11), they are "passed from death to life" (Jn. v.24; 1 Jn. III.14). In grasping all this, our sense of indebtedness to the sheer grace that has delivered us is to be deepened by the fact that in the death and sufferings of Jesus on the Cross, in the dereliction and torment of soul and heart that came on Him as He bore our sins, we see signs of the Hell, dereliction and damnation from which He has saved us in entering it Himself.

Now, therefore, the motive of all our behaviour must be a response to the love that has so freely liberated us from such a fate and such a bondage at so great a cost. We can no longer hope to begin to deserve through our obedience the great destiny marked out for the people of God. It was given to us before we deserved it. We, too, may have to continue to acknowledge ourselves like Israel, a people unreliable, unholy, unpredictable, impure. Yet God comes to us and says to us afresh every day, "I am the Lord thy God," calls on us to accept again the liberty He offers us, to live up to it in the light and power of His grace, walking in newness of life, because the very Word that commands us has the power to effect within us what it commands. "The Love of Christ constraineth us; because we thus judge that if one died for all, then were all dead: and that he died for all, that they which live should not henceforth live unto themselves, but unto him which died for them and rose again" (II Cor. v.14–15).

3. The direction of the life of liberty

The Ten Commandments are not merely a call to enter a life of liberty. They are meant to indicate the way of life that gives true expression to the glorious liberty in which the Children of God stand. When Paul said to the Galatians, "Ye have been called unto liberty; only use not liberty for an occasion to the flesh" (Gal. v.13), he was making the same kind of appeal to the Church of the New Testament as is here made in the

Commandments to Israel. It seems to be precisely the perverse-
ness of the "flesh" against which Paul is warning us, to want to
make of the Commandments a rigid set of rules binding men's
lives to a "law," so complete that when moral guidance is
required the grace of God can now be forgotten.

It must not seem far-fetched, therefore, to find many promises
hidden here within and under the form of the Commandments.
In their positive form they tell us the direction in which our life
can now move by the grace of God in maintaining and expressing the liberty which has been given to us. In their negative
form they tell us what is now unnecessary and impossible for
us, since God has now adopted us and given us a new status of
liberty. They say, "You do not need now to destroy and devour
each other, to give way to despair or to copy the heathen in their
way of life, to fall from the faith that can keep you from
idolatry and false worship, for when I am your God, I am
sufficient for you." They are ringing and positive claims by
God about the power of His grace and the glory of the liberty
He has given to us. In this sense they are a yoke that is easy and
a burden that is light.

We must try, then, to interpret them as an appeal to the
people of God to live according to the new relationship to Him
and to other men and to life, in which they have been placed
by His goodness in saving them. This takes us to the heart of
the New Testament teaching on what we sometimes call
"ethics." Here, all the appeals and commands that relate to our
behaviour in our daily life come after there has been some
exposition of the new relationship of liberty and grace in which
we now stand before man and God. Here, our attitude towards
our fellow man in every respect is controlled by the fact that
he too is one for whom Christ has died. Here, sloth, pride,
stealing, and smuttiness are banished, because the kingdom of
light has now replaced the kingdom of darkness. Here, sex is
discussed not in terms of some supposed virtue of chastity which
can be played off against another supposed virtue of charity,
but on the basis of the real and living relationship of man and
his members to the body of Christ who dwells in us and we in
Him. Here family relationships are looked on as being patterned
after the personal relationships within the mystery of the being

of God Himself, and in the relationship of Christ to His Church. Here, idolatry is regarded simply as an impossibility in the light of Christ's Lordship revealed in His death and resurrection. Here, justification by faith alone, apart from works, is seen to be the real meaning of the Sabbath day. Here, the whole can be summed up in a few short words: "Reckon ye also yourselves to be dead indeed unto sin, but alive unto God through Jesus Christ our Lord" (Rom. vi.11).

4. The personal word for the concrete situation

The Ten Commandments do not allow us to become lost in generalities. Nor do they allow us to criticise others too much before we criticise ourselves. They say to us, "Thou shalt do this. . . . Thou shalt not do that!" They make things personal, and they do not forget to ask us about our own conduct towards our neighbour. This prevents us from talking vaguely about Government failures or general moral standards, before we face the question of our own actual personal behaviour in those matters about which we love to generalise so much. When the prophet, John the Baptist, was sent by God to speak to King Herod about his evil way of life, John did not preach to Herod a sermon about some "absolute ideal of chastity." He did not speak generally about the evil of the times, making vague references to the eternal law of God. He did not even say, "It is wrong to commit adultery." He, rather, said flatly and decidedly in the name of God, "It is not lawful for *thee* to have *her*" (Mt. xiv.4). This is how the Ten Commandments seek to speak to us if we will listen to them. Through them we hear the voice of the living Lord, the Good Shepherd, addressing us in a thoroughly pointed and personal way about the concrete problems of our actual behaviour.

The Ten Commandments, then, usher us into a world dominated by a living Lord, who desires to enter personal communion with His people and to give personal guidance to them when they are in every situation involving moral decisions. Certainly there are plenty of rules and regulations in this world of the Ten Commandments. As they are set forth here, they are the summary and focal point of a mass of detailed legislation going into all kinds of cases often in minute detail. The Ten Commandments themselves are obviously meant to be understood in the light of much of the surrounding laws and rules applying to such particular cases. But even in the midst of all this mass of rules, and discussion of cases, the men of Israel were never to forget the living Lord who would be there to give them guidance, speaking directly to them as they faced the issues before them and the demands of His covenant. God made His people to depend for guidance, not primarily on the study of the book of the law, but on the living voice through which they would hear His word. As well as giving them the Law, He gave them Moses and the prophets to interpret and apply the Law afresh in the new situations of each generation. We read that He also gave them His "angel" to lead them in their perplexity (Ex. xxiii.20; xxxii.34; xxxiii.2). Whatever this means, it reinforces the fact that His guidance was to come often in a more living way than through a code book. It is also significant that at the very time when it became obvious to Moses that the Commandments by themselves were going to be hopelessly insufficient either to restrain or guide Israel in their sinfulness, God encouraged Moses with the promise: "My presence shall go with thee, and I will give thee rest" (Ex. xxxiii. 14).

We need such personal guidance from a living Lord. Life is too complicated for any set of rules and regulations, however well composed or however large and comprehensive, to fit into it at all relevantly. The human heart is too stubborn and subtle in its evil for vague ideals and principles to have any real power ultimately to control those decisions. Life is such that often the situation with which we are faced involves the breaking of one "commandment" in order to keep another, and often situations arise for which there is no real parallel in past history, and therefore very little moral tradition which can help us to find which way we must take.

The men of the Bible knew this well, and that is why we have them constantly telling God and men about the utter blindness and perplexity they felt, even with all their knowledge of God's law, as they stood in the middle of the path along which God was leading them and their nation and sought His guidance on moral, political, and personal problems of every kind. This is why Israel is described as a "blind people that have eyes" and a "deaf that have ears," being brought through their life-situations by God's personal care (Is. XLIII.8). This is why the psalmist writes the prayer "I am a stranger in the earth; hide not thy commandments from me" (Ps. CXIX.19; II Chron. XX.12). Even though they had the deepest possible understanding of the mind of the Lord as it could be expressed in His Law, and were thoroughly versed in the details of His legislation, they knew they needed something more—the living Lord Himself speaking a new word in their constantly changing situation. They steadied themselves on the fact that they had been promised such a word: "Thine ears shall hear a word behind thee, saying, this is the way, walk ye in it" (Is. XXX.21). But they knew that this word for which they prayed and hoped would be no more than a light to their path and a lamp to their feet (Ps. CXIX.105), showing simply one step at a time, as it ever gave fresh illumination.

All this must apply even more forcibly to life today than it did in the days of the Old Testament. The moral, political, and social problems of today are even more complicated than those of an age that knew neither nuclear bombs, nor football pools, nor artificial means of contraception and insemination, nor tobacco, nor psychoanalysis, nor mass media of communication. St Luke tells us that the risen Lord drew near to the two disciples on the road to Emmaeus, and "beginning at Moses and all the prophets he expounded unto them in all the Scriptures the things concerning himself" (Lk. XXIV.27). This story is relevant when we are seeking to understand what the Ten Commandments have to say to us today in our present situation. What we will find in them is not a set of principles or ideals, but the will of Him who is the Lord of the Church, and the Lord of our situation in the world, who speaks so that His sheep hear His voice (Jn. X.27), and who in speaking draws near to men Himself and calls on them to follow Him on the way through which He is leading His Church. It pleases Him to use these, and all scriptures, to bring us light on His will for us today. But He ever has been, and remains, Lord of the Scriptures. It is through Him that we understand them, even though it is through them that we come to know Him and His mind.

Certainly there is some danger in this approach. We would feel more secure if we were able simply to map out our way beforehand with very hard and fast arguments from a very clear and comprehensive moral code. But we too have to learn even in the sphere of morals to "walk by faith and not by sight" (II Cor. v.7), and like the men of the Old Testament to become blind in order to see, knowing that to the upright "there ariseth light in the darkness" (Ps. CXII.4).

5. The call to self-denial

If we are to understand the Ten Commandments we must be prepared to take seriously the significance of their negative form. Far too often the fact that many of them begin with the phrase "thou shalt not . . ." has been regarded as a defect, and is often criticised in a superficial way.

In their negative form the Commandments must have been a sharp reminder to Israel of the difference that must appear between the way of life of the people of God and the way of life of other nations, and a call to restrain the very tendencies that had been allowed to mark the life of other nations with so much that was displeasing to God.

For us the negative form of the Commandments brings primarily a call to restraint. It reminds us that the enemy is within us as well as around us. We are commanded not to do certain things because God knows, as well as we do, that we have within us a tendency to do these things, even if we are not doing them. Our sin in this matter may be hidden and respectable, but it is nevertheless real. It was to this that Jesus was referring when He pointed out that the hatred of the heart was indeed murder, and the lustful thought was indeed adultery (Mt. v.21–8). The negative form of the Commandments is due to the fact that they are more closely related to life as it is, than much of our present-day out-worn idealistic moralising.

Therefore the Commandments can bring us to the place where we learn one of our first lessons in living the Christian life. They remind us that we must restrain, by the power of the living Christ, what is ineradicably there in the human heart, and be honest about it. When Jesus, obviously interpreting the Ten Commandments, said, "Out of the heart proceed evil thoughts, murders, adulteries, fornications, thefts, false witness, blasphemies" (Mt. xv.19), He was speaking for the twentieth century as much as for the first. When He said "If any man will come after me, let him deny himself" (Mt. xvi.24), He was referring to this need for a ruthless, radical, self-restraint on all the issues on which we are challenged by the Commandments. The same need is re-echoed by Paul in his wonderful description of love in the thirteenth chapter of his first epistle to the Corinthians. ("Love envieth not . . . not . . . not . . ." etc.) By bringing before us the secrets of our hearts in this way, the Commandments keep us from setting ourselves up as judges of others.

6. The relevance of the whole Gospel
for the whole of life

In their actual details the Commandments say little. They can be very quickly read. In themselves they raise more questions than they answer. Yet the vastness of their scope is remarkable; through them God claimed for His service every aspect of the life of the people He had brought out of bondage. On whatever their concern might be, at home, in the temple, in the market place, in the inner chambers, in the secrets of their hearts, in their journeyings, their resting, their work, their leisure, and on all the relationships in which they might be involved with their fellow men, God laid His hand and said, "It is here that you must listen to My voice. It is here that you are to live by the grace that has liberated you, and express your new-found freedom!"

The Commandments today remind us in the same way of God's concern that every aspect of our human life should be brought under the control of His Word. The fact that we can easily grasp them as a whole, and recognise the place that each Commandment has within the whole, will keep us either from over-emphasising or from neglecting any one aspect of the moral life. The Commandments, for example, force us to deal with sex, but they also save us from giving way to any Freudian suggestion that the discussion of sex should have any place of priority in our attention. They force us to face the problem of nuclear disarmament, but they prevent us from being so apocalyptic as to say that only this problem matters. They force us to remember that love towards God must have priority over, and yet must be followed by, love towards our neighbour.

We cannot forget that the Commandments, even as we have them in the Pentateuch, are surrounded by a mass of other legislation which acts like a commentary on them. They were meant to be understood in the light of the whole corpus of the Law. Today we must seek to understand them in the light of the teaching of the whole Bible.

Of course they will probably say more, and perhaps different things, to us than they said to former generations. The Commandment "Thou shalt not steal" said much more to the landed proprietors who listened to the preaching of the prophets of the 6th century B.C. than it did to the generation which followed Moses in the wilderness. What the Commandment about the Sabbath said to the Church in 1864 does not altogether apply in 1964. The Commandment "Thou shalt not kill" is bound to have a more disturbing effect on our will to go to war in a nuclear age than it did in 1939. Indeed, it is possible that where hitherto a Commandment has not been heard categorically to forbid, it might now be heard to this precise effect.

We must avoid, above all, making the Commandments into a string of rigid rules, clearly and once-for-all defining a way of behaviour which must remain hard and fast throughout all ages. They must become to us rather the focus through which the light of the whole Bible can fall in a living, penetrating, and compelling way upon the path which we must take, so that light enough will be given us in our immediate situation to enable us to take the next step by faith in our unplanned journey of life.

7. "A light to the Gentiles"

The keeping of the Commandments was meant to make Israel a "light to the Gentiles" (Is. XLIX.6). As they gave expression, within their social and family life, to the liberty into

which they were called and empowered by the grace of God
and directed by His Commandments, their way of life was to
set a pattern of which other nations would take notice. The
Gentile nations could not be expected directly to heed the
actual Commandments given to Israel. These were addressed
to the redeemed people. But the Gentile nations were bound to
heed the existence of a true Israel in the midst, and to open
their eyes to the fact that here was a light shining in the darkness, offering them guidance in a way that was unique, true,
righteous, and worth following. Even the Gentiles were to
re-echo the words of their greatest prophets, "For what nation
is there so great, who hath God so nigh unto them, as the Lord
our God is in all things that we call upon him for? And what
nation is there so great, that hath statutes and judgments so
righteous as all this law which I set before you this day?"
(Deut. IV.7–8; cp. XXXIII.29).

It is in this way that the Ten Commandments, interpreted
primarily as a word of liberation and direction to the people
of God within the Church of today, are to be given relevance
for the world which still exists outside the Church, and for the
State which still confronts the Church and has to take note of
the Church in its midst, whether it be a large and powerful
Church, or a small minority body. The easiest way, of course,
to apply the Ten Commandments to those outside the Church
is to turn them into natural laws or general moral principles
and proclaim their relevance for all men since the God of Israel
who gave them is the God of the whole earth. But this does not
meet the situation, and it does not convince, in any powerful
way whatever, the attitude of mind and the outlook which the
Church has to face. The Ten Commandments are intended to
point us constantly to the pattern to which the life of the people
of God will tend to conform as they seek to live by faith, and
express their gratitude to the redeeming Lord, in the concrete
situations of modern life. They will be enabled to fulfil this
pattern by the same grace as has once-for-all redeemed them
and given them this new freedom within modern life. But this
pattern of new life which we see first of all fulfilled in Jesus
Christ before it is reflected in the Church's life, is indeed the
truth for all men. It is a pattern which reveals anew the mean-

ing of our creation and the meaning of all human destiny. To make it relevant as a possibility for all men to hold before themselves, Jesus Christ has poured out His spirit upon all flesh, and has entered a new relationship even with those who do not yet confess His name. Even for them, still living in alienation from Him, the pattern of His earthly life and His Church's life has the utmost significance as a guiding light within their fearful darkness, and along with this gift there is given through the presence of the Church in the midst, a stabilising and healing influence which they will do well not to reject.

THE FIRST COMMANDMENT

EXODUS xx. 2–6. *I am the Lord thy God, which have brought thee out of the land of Egypt, out of the house of bondage. Thou shalt have no other gods before me.*

CHAPTER I

THE ULTIMATE CHOICE

1. A strange and dangerous possibility

As we read through the Bible it becomes clear that God never excluded from His people's lives the possibility of forsaking Him for others. At every stage of their history they were free to give their worship, and pour out the service of their lives, to gods other than Himself. The world through which they passed, and in the midst of which they eventually settled down in Canaan, was always to them a dangerous world of idols. And for some strange reason, they often preferred to deal with such idols rather than with the living God. From their earliest days they had been idolators. When Joshua, at a critical stage in their history, pled with them to "put away the gods which your fathers served on the other side of the flood, and in Egypt" (Josh. xxiv.14), he was attacking a perpetual characteristic of their national life. And when they entered the promised land it was only after a fierce and critical struggle that their loyalty to God survived the fascination of idols like Dagon, Baal, Chemosh, Ashtaroth, and a multitude of lesser members of the local Pantheon.

"There be gods many and lords many", wrote Paul, centuries later to the Church in Corinth (1 Cor. viii.5). He was thinking not only of the situation that faced his forbears in the Old Testament world. He was looking back on his own experience when, on his arrival in Athens, even he was astonished at the multitude of idols, one in every corner of every street, and his spirit was "stirred within him when he saw the city wholly given to idolatry" (Acts xvii.16). He was also thinking of the situation facing each young Christian Church of his day in the same dangerous world of idols.

2. The significance and power of the idol

The danger in this situation lay not simply in the actual physical presence of a multitude of idols and shrines, inviting acts of worship. The idol stood for the way of life of the people who worshipped it, a way of life that was always incompatible with that set before them in the covenant which the Lord God of Israel had made with His people. It was universally recognised that the act of bowing down to the idol implied the surrender of heart and mind and soul to the alien culture and way of life for which it stood.

When Joshua, in pleading with Israel to put away their idols, called them "strange Gods," he meant that they were gods whose very worship implied a "strange" way of life, alien to that to which the Lord had called them (Josh. xxiv.23). When Nebuchadnezzar the Babylonian Emperor, in his desire for absolute power in a unified community, wanted to absorb his captive peoples into the Babylonian ways of life, he was not content simply to give them Babylonian names, and to introduce them superficially to Babylonian education, culture, and ways of feeding. He had also to set up a colossal Babylonian idol, embodying all that Babylon stood for, and to decree that every one of his subjects should fall down and worship it, to the accompaniment of suitable Babylonian music (Dan. iii.1–5). Earlier in the history of Israel, Jezebel the daughter of the king of Tyre had followed the same policy under the same conviction. After her marriage with Ahab, King of Israel, she went to her new homeland determined to change its way of life, its economics, its land-laws, its class structure, in order to make them more like those of her father's kingdom of Tyre. Her policy was to build in Samaria a temple to Baal, the God of Tyre, to import six hundred priests of the cult of Baal, and to tempt Israel to substitute the worship of Baal for that of the Lord. Through such idolatry, both Nebuchadnezzar and Jezebel really wanted of Israel not simply a superficial act of compromising religious conformity, but a sign that they were ready to give up their covenanted way of life, and no longer determined to remain the peculiar people, with unique ways, belonging to a God who would allow no other influence but His own to mould them.

All the spiritual leaders of Israel in their day recognised the fatal and dangerous compromise that was signified and involved when their nation gave way to any form of idolatry. In their view the idol exercised power over those who worshipped it. It was not simply a visible object of aesthetic value, it was also the focal point of a real spiritual force that could dominate men and communities, and hold them in bondage.

Here, then, in the First Commandment, we are faced with an issue of life or death for the people of God. It is a warning against falling back into an outlook, a bondage of heart and mind, from which they have been once-for-all delivered by what God has done for them in His love. The warning is repeated again and again in the New Testament. "Flee from idolatry" (1 Cor. x.14), writes Paul to the Corinthians. Certainly he knew that an idol in itself was "nothing in the world" (1 Cor. viii.4). Yet in this matter he feels himself engaged in a struggle to save his people from slipping back into the "power" (1 Cor. vi.12) of a way of life which could cause their weak members to "perish" (1 Cor. viii.11). "Simon, Simon," said Jesus, "behold, Satan hath desired to have you, that he may sift you as wheat: But I have prayed for thee, that thy faith fail not" (Lk. xxii.31).

3. The gods around us today

Do we not still live today in the midst of this dangerous world of idols? Certainly there are few of the shrines of the traditional pagan deities in our midst. Commercial advertisements in our streets take the place which altars and idols took in the Greek and Roman cities of the past. But a Hitler has only to arise and thrust himself in the place the idol has occupied in the history of all pagan religions, and a whole nation's way of life and worship becomes distorted. In such a quiet and simple way a false God, with power to destroy, can suddenly appear in our modern sophisticated world! Christians who have lived in East Germany in recent years have felt with terrible intensity that their own state, in its zeal to conform all men to one way of life and thinking, has been again turning itself into an idol and claiming, especially from children and young people, a devotion that cuts right across the obedience a Christian is bound to give to this Commandment. In the midst of this they feel that they are again being confronted by powers that are seeking to destroy their devotion to Christ.

We may be sheltered from such blatant idolatrous claims being made upon us in the political sphere by blustering dictators, but we are nevertheless being constantly and ruthlessly accosted by the claims and lures of false gods in other forms. They accost us in the form of some of the political, social, cultural, or business forces and pressures in which men can become involved as they go about their daily work in our modern society, and participate in its culture and amusement. In the long run in yielding to these pressures we can become compelled to slacken our loyalty to God as we know Him in Jesus Christ, and can allow our life to become dominated by something other than the love that has redeemed us. John's words are still relevant: "Love not the world, neither the things that are in the world. If any man love the world the love of the Father is not in him. For all that is in the world, the lust of the flesh, and the lust of the eyes, and the pride of life, is not of the Father, but is of the world" (1 Jn. 11.15–16). We too can be carried away irrationally, by forces and enticements as strong and imperious as any that held the Children of Israel in Egypt, and from which God had to bring them out with mighty power and outstretched arm. The cult of sex, and the cult of personality, and the worship of money, stimulated by all the techniques which modern science has put at our disposal, and sublimated only a little from their crasser ancient forms, are no less idolatrous forces in modern life than they were when they were centred on the altars of Venus or Bacchus or Mammon, and the God Mars seems to be preparing an altar more copious than ever before, for the sacrifice of the masses who are willing to allow themselves to be led into following him.

Even the pathetic Old Testament stories of the little private gods which pious Israelites kept hidden in their household baggage, could easily be paralleled in modern life. Luther once said "truly, whatever thy heart clings to and trusts in, that is properly thy God." The heart still clings easily and naturally to whatever impressively thrusts itself forward on the stage of life or history with a superficial show of strength and a few superficial promises. It responds quickly to alien claims, with a service, devotion and loyalty that should be kept for God alone. The strange and terrible possibility is still within us and open before us, that we might allow ourselves to become so gripped and impressed by causes, programmes, personalities and philosophies alien to the living God, and to the way of life and thinking to which we are called in His Word, that we come to have other gods before Him.

4. The exposure of the sham

"I am the Lord thy God which brought thee out of the land of Egypt, out of the house of bondage." The children of Israel were a people before whose eyes God had already fully exposed the emptiness and stupidity of all idolatry. In their minds their captivity in Egypt had been captivity under the power of the idol. Their bondage had been bondage to the gods of Egypt. These gods had seemed mighty, indeed, as they had groaned under their power. The culture which their worship inspired seemed imposing and enduring—and Pharoah, with his harsh and irrevocable demands, was the embodiment of the word of power that went forth from them.

And yet all this had collapsed, and that with startling suddenness, before the authority of the word spoken by Moses in the name of the Lord who had chosen Abraham, Isaac, Jacob, and their seed to be the people through whom the whole earth was to be blessed. The power and victory of the Lord had destroyed for ever the might of Pharoah and revealed its sham. They had seen with their own eyes all the Egyptians hastening to their own death, sinking like lead in the mighty waters, and finally scattered upon the sea-shore, lifeless. Now they knew that all that the Lord spoke in judgment on the idols of this world must come to pass. Now Moses could proclaim to them as an indisputable fact of their own history, and as an elementary lesson from their own experience that "the Lord, he is God in heaven above and in the earth beneath: there is none else" (Deut. IV.39).

The later prophets could remind every succeeding generation of the same facts and the same truth. "I am the Lord, and there is none else, there is no God beside me" (Is. XLV.5). Now, for ever, Israel must believe that no way of life that was not

centred on Him, could bring any satisfaction or real fruitfulness, that no worship, directed otherwise than to Him alone,
could have any reality and truth, and that everything that
proved itself strange and alien when He was in the midst,
must be a lie and a delusion of evil. A typical story of the Old
Testament is that of the Ark of the Lord having been captured
by the Philistines and put in the temple of Dagon in the presence
of the Philistine idols, only to result in the Philistine idols being
found flattened and mutilated as if by some unseen divine
power, in the presence of the awe-inspiring Ark. The Lord
alone was real. Every idol was vain.

The New Testament shows us Jesus Christ as Lord in the
midst of the idols, in the same decisive way. He is shown as the
One who by His coming, life, teaching, death, and resurrection
has exposed the shams of the open or secret idolatries that men
can slip into if they are conformed to this world and its ways.
As the disciples looked back over His career on this earth and
thought out its meaning in the light of His resurrection and
ascension, they recognised that the forces which had opposed
Jesus could be described simply as the gods of this world, and
could be identified with the powers that had gained their hold
over men through the world's idolatry in every age, whatever
its form might be. It was these powers that Jesus had challenged
to battle in opposing the society of His day, and between them
and Him the struggle had been the one decisive battle of all
time for authority over men.

As a man, Jesus lived all his life completely as an offering of
service to the One God, His heavenly Father. He rejected the
temptation in the wilderness to win the world by compromising
with its idolatry, and bowing down to the one who seemed to
have power everywhere. It was because of this that He found
Himself inevitably involved in a sea of conflict, and in such
opposition to all the "powers" and ways around Him that
ultimately He allowed Himself to die alone at their hands. His
death gave them their greatest show of triumph. But in the
very moment of their triumph He had risen again, proved
Himself their conqueror, and shown up for ever the emptiness
of all their claims, aims, and rewards. Paul puts it this way:
"having spoiled principalities and powers, he made a shew of

them openly, triumphing over them in it" (Col. II.15). And with this fact in mind he reinforces his appeal to the members of the Corinthian Church to flee from idolatry: "We know that an idol is nothing in the world, and that there is none other God but one. For though there be that are called gods, whether in heaven or in earth . . . to us there is but one God" (1 Cor. VIII.4–5). How could there be any other but one God, to men who had seen Him at work so victoriously in Jesus?

There can be only one decisive battle in this warfare between the true God and the power of idolatry. It was the vanity of the idolatry of our own age no less than that of the world of the first century, that was exposed once-for-all in the conflict and victory of Jesus over the powers of darkness. We do not require another coming of a Christ, another gospel drama, another cross and resurrection either to redeem us afresh today or to judge again the evil of the world. "By one offering" Jesus has done it for us once-for-all (Heb. x.14). All men in every age are therefore now delivered from the fascination and drawing-power of the "prince of this world," and are free to yield to the drawing-power which the Cross will exercise in every age. This is His claim and promise for each of us, as well as for the men of His own earthly day: "Now is the judgment of this world. Now shall the prince of this world be cast out. And I, if I be lifted up from the earth, will draw all men unto me" (Jn. XII.31–2). All that is required to expose the sham of the idols of today and to destroy their power to hold the hearts of men, is the "lifting up" of the Cross so that the exalted and ever-living Lord can exercise through it the influence that He has won the right to have over the minds and hearts of all men. Now in the light of His Cross, men will know the power of His victory as a reality beginning to be fulfilled even in their daily lives. When the crucified, risen, and exalted Christ is proclaimed to men in the twentieth century, the power of our modern idolatry in the hearts of men is "cast out".

5. Command and promise

This Commandment, as we have seen, comes to us today primarily as a promise. The "casting out" of the subtle seducing-power of our modern idols, takes place through the sheer grace and power of Christ, and not through our own efforts.

But, since the Commandment is based on so firm a promise, obedience to it does become the most urgent matter facing any individual, or group, or nation on earth. Here we are given the command of One who will brook no rival. Whatever other honour or deference we seek to pay to Him means nothing, if at the same time we seek to place, in our loyalty and affections, something else alongside of Him. "No man can serve two masters," Jesus said, referring precisely to the conflict which can take place on this supreme level of life, "for either he will hate the one and love the other; or else he will hold to the one and despise the other" (Mt. vi.14). In loving and holding to God, we must deliberately hate and despise everything else that could possibly become a counter-influence, slackening our loyalty in this sphere. To us, He alone must be Lord. Nothing must be compared with Him, or mentioned alongside of Him, when the basis, aim, and hopes of our life are in question. He alone has to be feared and obeyed and loved in an unqualified way with all our heart and with all our strength and with all our mind and with all our soul (Lk. x.27–8; Deut. vi.4). His judgment in all things is to be accepted with faith and gratitude, for He alone has the right to command and dispose without possibility of argument and without need to appeal. It was the imperious nature of this Commandment that was in the mind of Peter and the other Apostles, when in the face of possible martyrdom for continuing to teach and preach in the name of Jesus, they refused to draw back, saying, "We ought to obey God, rather than men" (Acts v.29).

But Peter and his companions could not have risen to such heights of courageous obedience to the command unless they had had the glowing certainty in their heart that those who trusted Christ to the extent of the martyrdom that threatened them, would never lose their reward and never be forsaken. What we are asked for here, is not the slavish obedience of the terrified, but the confident response of grateful and adoring faith that has seen not only that alongside of God there is no other, but also that there is no need for another.

The New Testament shows us a Christ who gives all before He commands all, and who commands all, only because He first gives all. The First Commandment finds its truest New Testament form in the words of Jesus: "Come unto me all ye that labour and are heavy laden, and I will give you rest. Take my yoke upon you, and learn of me: for I am meek and lowly in heart: and ye shall find rest unto your souls" (Mt. xi.28–9). And this is re-echoed by Paul, time and again: "In him dwelleth all the fulness of the Godhead bodily. And ye are complete in him" (Col. ii.9–10). "Christ Jesus, who of God is made unto us wisdom, and righteousness, and sanctification, and redemption" (1 Cor. 1.30). It is because so much is given us in Christ to be the ground of our faith, the centre of our worship, and the source of our forgiveness and new life, that it is an absurd and insulting denial of the love that has given it, to turn away and look elsewhere for something else.

Yet sometimes we Christians behave as if what we have in Christ is only partial, and has to be supplemented through what we find in other sources of wisdom, knowledge, inspiration, and strength. In order to supplement our knowledge of God we will turn to a philosophy that has no conceivable connexion with the revelation we are given of Jesus Christ in the Scripture. In order to enrich our spirits, and to find a new meaning and deeper satisfaction in this life, we will turn to purely humanistic culture for a fresh source of inspiration. When we are faced with the tragedy of bereavement we will turn to spiritualistic media in order to try to add something to our knowledge of the hereafter that we feel is lacking in our Christian faith. And when we are faced with the ultimate problem of human guilt before God we are tempted to try psychological means of solving it, in preference to the means that Christ has given us of communion with Himself in Word and Sacrament.

Certainly there must be a high and real place in human life for philosophy, for science, for psychology, and for the contemplation and admiration of the wonders of nature. How can we be so boorish as to refuse to rejoice in whatsoever things are good, true, just, and lovely? (Phil. iv.8). But when it is a question of the ground of our faith, the centre of our worship,

the source of the forgiveness of our sins, and the finding of the
ultimate purpose and satisfaction of our lives, this high and
real place must not be anywhere near the place given to Jesus
Christ. Nothing must stand beside Him, in His work of revealing God, cleansing from sin and enabling our hearts to find
their true destiny. We can turn to nature, to our philosophy,
to our social and cultural pursuits, to the service of our fellow
men, only as those who have already found in Christ their God,
and who need no other to stand or to work alongside of Him
in His saving, cleansing, and revealing work as God. In all else
we see simply the unfolding of a fulness that we have already
acknowledged to be in Him. We make nothing else a source of
anything that can be new and vital, but we use all else as in
thankfulness to Him in whom we have found all. Can anything
less be a true response to the First Commandment?

6. A call to faith

This command can be summed up as a call to faith. To have
faith in God is so to commit oneself to God that one has no
other object of trust and no other source of inspiration and life
that can possibly now in any way interfere with this total
committment. To have faith in God is to cling to God in such
a way that every other support must be forsaken in the act of
laying hold of Him. It is therefore the simple act of believing
in God that is really the complete fulfilment of this first commandment, which God expects from us. If we believe in God
at all, we believe in God alone, for faith can have only one
object of trust. No one has put the issue more clearly than
Jeremiah. "Thus saith the Lord: Cursed be the man that
trusteth in man, and maketh the flesh the arm, and whose
heart departeth from the Lord" (Jer. xvii.5). If a man tries to
trust in anything else besides God alone, it is not as if he has
injured his faith and hurt God somewhat, it is actually that he
has dishonoured God and departed entirely from Him.

But how are we to come to such faith as will honour God
by keeping this Commandment? We must look again to Him
whose promises cover all our need, to create within our heart
the very faith they call forth. We must listen again to these

never failing promises, and realise that they are the Word of One to whom all power is given in heaven and in earth, and who has proved once and for ever that besides Himself there cannot possibly be another.

THE SECOND COMMANDMENT

EXODUS xx.4–6. *Thou shalt not make unto thee any graven image, or any likeness of anything that is in the heaven above, or that is in the earth beneath, or that is in the water under the earth: thou shalt not bow down thyself to them nor serve them: for I the Lord thy God am a jealous God, visiting the iniquity of the fathers upon the children unto the third and fourth generation of them that hate me; and showing mercy unto thousands of them that love me, and keep my commandments.*

CHAPTER II

THE IMAGE OF THE INVISIBLE GOD

1. The importance of words in the service of God

BETWEEN man and man, words are powerful things. They can be a means of fellowship. Through them we can give form and expression to our desires and thoughts, and utter what is in our minds and hearts so that others can understand and come to know us.

Between God and man, words can be even more significant and powerful. The Bible story of the dealings of God with His people, shows us that God has always used words, in communicating Himself, His mind, and His will, to men. Time and again we read such phrases as, "The word of the Lord came . . .," or "God spoke and said. . . ." It is deeply significant that at the very start of the Bible story we are introduced to God in the act of creating life and order by speaking: "And God said Let there be . . . and there was" (Gen. 1.3). Indeed, in the Bible it is a wonderful miracle of love that the invisible God, who reigns in light inaccessible, should nevertheless, in spite of the distance between Creator and creature, between the Holy One and sinners, be willing and able to express His will and communicate His love, blessing and life to them in this way. The whole structure of the life of the Church today witnesses to the fact that God still uses words to communicate with us. We have the Bible, given its rightful place of honour in the Church as the main means of our coming to know Him and entering His presence. We have the preaching of the Word as the main sacrament at the heart of the Church's Life.

Those who were with Jesus during His earthly life tell us in the Gospels that He constantly used words, and often used little else than words, in forgiving, healing, and blessing men. He has not changed. He still, today, uses words more than anything else, not simply to indicate to us what His will is, but also to convey to us His gift of forgiveness and new life. He

once spoke parables indicating that as seeds convey to the
earth the life and possibilities of a growing new harvest, so
His words preached to the minds and hearts of men would
convey into the midst of this world's life the power and reality
of the new creation which it was His life's work to bring in
(Cp. Mt. xiii). Words are still a means by which the living
Christ conveys the power and life of His kingdom into the
lives of men within the Church today.

2. The importance of images in the service of God

"He knoweth our frame" says the psalmist (Ps. ciii.14).
He knows that the human mind can be even more quickly
impressed by images than by words—no matter how great and
sublime are the ideas conveyed by such words. It creates images
of what it wants to hold before it. If it is not given a true image
of a thing it will form a false image. Therefore God, in His
love, does not confine Himself only to communicating with
men and having fellowship with them through speech. He
approaches man with images of Himself that are as true to
Himself as possible, and concrete enough for life, images that
man can grasp and take into his mind to form the centre of
his thinking and devotion. Even early in the Old Testament
history we have occasional visions of God given to men either
in dreams or during waking hours. God well knows that we
have eyes as well as ears, and that our minds think in terms of
things we can "visualise" as well as conceive in other ways.

This Second Commandment is there to remind us of the
importance of such images in the service of God. "Thou shalt
not make unto thee any graven image. . . ." This does not mean,
"You must never have an image of God to bow down before,
or to make the centre of your worship and adoration." It
means rather that God reserves for Himself alone the right to
express and produce the images of Himself before which men
must worship, through which men must conceive Him, to
which men must respond in obedience to His own initiative in
seeking fellowship with them.

Therefore God really desires to enter into the cravings for a
visible representation of Himself which makes the heathen carve

their images with such love, and makes the Christians of many denominations of today want to fill their Churches with statues imagery, and visible symbols. It is as if God said, "I am going to give them something real and genuine to replace the unreality of all their own religious images and creations. I will give them an image which will indeed signify my true nature, and my real presence in the midst of those who meet to worship me and to serve me." God wants to be our God in every way. Therefore He delights to give Himself an image which indeed will satisfy the human yearning to see Him and to grasp His reality, and He has given Himself wholly to the creation of such an image.

good text to use Col.

3. The only true image of the invisible God

We can speak as we have been doing, about God's willingness and concern to communicate with us through the world of our imagery, only because the God we know in Jesus Christ has indeed expressed Himself exactly and truly in such an image. Jesus Christ is the "image of the invisible God" (Col. 1.15). In Him God has "become flesh," and in this way has made Himself visible. He has taken upon Himself a form that men can see and encounter and grasp. It is a fundamental thought of the Bible that all the occasional and fleeting Old Testament "visions" given by God of Himself, and the images chosen to represent Him, were all designed simply to serve and submit to this one image of the invisible God which was yet to appear in Jesus Christ.

The final image which we have of God in Jesus Christ is a true image. The image we have of Him, born in weakness, nursed at His mother's breast, growing within a family life in order to become like us in everything that happens to us, is a true image of the humility of the eternal God. The image we have of Him identifying Himself with sinners at His baptism, consorting with publicans and outcasts, is a true image of the seeking love of the eternal God for all men, and of His willingness to take their sin in His own heart. The picture we have of Him praying to the Father, communing in love with Him, finding consolation and strength in Him, is a true image of the fellowship which is, and was, and ever shall be, within the very being of His Godhead. The sight we have of Him healing the sick, stilling the storms, raising the dead, overcoming all His enemies with love, finishing the power and dominion of evil through the sacrifice of His cross, rising again after apparent defeat, and using the work of the devil to further His own purposes—all this is a true image of what philosophers sometimes have called the omnipotence of God. In this way we could go on and on, speaking about what God is, from what we find Jesus to be. "He that hath seen me hath seen the father" (Jn. xiv.9). "No man hath seen God at any time: the only begotten Son, which is in the bosom of the father, he hath declared Him" (Jn. 1.18).

The image which we have been given of God in Jesus Christ is the image of what lies deepest in the heart of the being of God. It is the image of what God expresses to Himself, within Himself and through Himself. When we speak of God as being the Holy Trinity, Father, Son, and Holy Spirit, we mean that God in the very depths of His being expresses Himself, in and through Himself. It lies in His inmost nature to express Himself. But in His love, He is not content to express Himself in this way only within Himself. His very desire to create the world means that He wills to express Himself outside of Himself, and in the coming of Jesus we have the complete outward expression of what God is to Himself and within Himself. In Him, indeed, we have an image that really corresponds to what is, and shall be for ever within the invisible heart of God. It is an image in which God really, as it were, turns Himself inside out, so that we may see what is there. In giving it to us, God is not merely selecting certain features in something else that distantly indicate something that is there in Himself, God Himself is active, rather, unveiling Himself for what He is.

The image which God gives us of Himself in Jesus Christ also really presents what it truly represents. It is reality as well as truth. It is what it speaks about. God gives us this image not simply in order that we might think of Him properly, and thus become stirred up with good and warm devotional feelings towards Him, but also in order that we might meet Him and commune with Him, so that He can for ever make His image

We are to be His image in word.

a meeting point with us for salvation and judgment. As we seek Him in faith, prayer, and worship, think of Him in terms of this image, set Him before us as He has expressed Himself and wills to express Himself to us in the Gospel of Christ, He will give us His presence, speak to us, commune with us, and bring to us His grace and judgment. Thus the image of God in Jesus mediates not only ideas about God, but God's very presence in the midst.

4. The service of the image by Word and Sacrament

If Jesus Christ is the image of the invisible God in flesh and blood in the complete and absolute way we have already affirmed, then all our imagery of thought and symbol must serve this image as did that of the Old Testament. We are now forbidden any other image. We cannot now pick and choose our own symbols of God, and say, "This and that will do!" If through the re-presentation of this image to the minds and thoughts of the people of God, God really gives His living presence today, then we must seek to make this image as real as possible to men today, and as relevant as possible. We must be rid of all false imagery. Indeed we must abhor that falsehood or distortion should enter here. Here is where the Second Commandment becomes relevant and urgent in modern Church life.

But how are we to put across, for today, this image of God we have been given in Jesus in such a way that God Himself will honour it and give His presence along with the image as we present it?

Many people today complain that there is a large element of falsehood in what the Bible presents to us as the image of God in its picture of Jesus Christ. In the much discussed book *Honest to God*, the Bishop of Woolwich has complained that for many people in England the possibility of a true faith is vitiated today because the Church is still, perhaps unconsciously, clinging to the images of God which it has inherited through its traditional interpretation of the Bible. It is asserted that one of these outdated images still in the popular Church mind is of God as "the old man in the sky" which is a hang-over from the days when men thought in terms of a three-decker universe, heaven above, the earth in the middle, and hell below. Similarly, another outdated image is that of God as a "super being" who comes from "beyond" the sphere of this world, to go through a salvation drama—an image encouraged by our traditional use of the Christmas story. Another undesirable image, according to the Bishop, is given to us in the account of the ascension of Jesus in the Gospels. To the Bishop and many others, such images are completely out of date in an age when space flights have destroyed the possibility of our being able to imagine a God who is literally up in the skies, or beyond anything. They feel that we must purge such pictures out of the imagery which the Bible gives us, if we are to be left with a true image of God.

Others complain that the image of God in Jesus, as we have it in the Bible, has not been vividly enough preserved in order to be a really powerful factor in our lives. Thomas Carlyle is reported as having once said to Holman Hunt: "I am only a poor man, but I can say in serious truth that I would give one third of all I possess for a veritable contemporaneous likeness of Christ. . . . Had these carvers of marble chiselled a faithful statue of the Son of Man, as he called Himself, and showed us what manner of man He was like, what His height, what His build, and what the features of His sorrow-marked face were, and what His dress, I, for one, would have thanked the sculptor with all the gratitude of my heart for that portrait, as the most precious heirloom of the ages." Today we could express the same feeling in a wish that there had been in Palestine of the time of Jesus a good film studio that had been able to produce reliable documentaries of contemporary events.

But God has made ample provision for the image which He has given of Himself in Jesus Christ to be preserved and represented to men of every age. For this purpose He did not bring in sculptors or artists. He enlisted first of all the service of faithful Prophets and writers before Christ came at all, the service of the men who wrote the Old Testament. And then He enlisted the service of faithful Apostles and writers of the New Testament.

These men knew the true form and meaning the image

which God gave of Himself in Christ, better than we do, for they were "on the spot" as it were, when it happened, and they were inspired by the Spirit to understand it and to witness to it. It is through their words and witness that we have presented to us today the image of Jesus Christ that is to stand all through the ages in the Church as the main source through which we must find the image of God. And, today, to reproduce this image for our time, God enlists, not the service of museum curators or art collectors, not that of film distributors but that of simple preachers of the Gospel, chosen and called by Him and trained by His Church, and inspired also by His Spirit, and set the task of studying the Scripture in order to reproduce for our day and generation what was given once-for-all in Jesus Christ.

To be able to reproduce the full image which God has given us of Himself in Jesus Christ we need both the Old and the New Testaments. In the Old Testament God through the visions and messages He gave, through the historical experiences through which He put His people, and through the interpretation of these experiences, showed His people then, and us today, how Jesus was to be understood when He came. He showed how Jesus' life and death were to be interpreted, and what features of His life and work and teaching were to be the most significant for the image He had to present to us. All the other images and words of God in the Old Testament were meant to give a faint sketchy outline, such as would prepare men for the ultimate revelation of the true image, and would help them and us to understand and interpret it. The New Testament is simply the setting forth of the image as the Apostles saw it, interpreted in the light of the Old Testament, and as they want us to see it today.

But God is concerned to leave us with more than a book and a ministry for the re-presentation of His image before us today. Before He removed His visible bodily presence from men, Jesus gave the Church two very simple, and in themselves deeply impressive, images of Himself in Baptism and the Lord's Supper. While these two sacraments primarily serve to bring us into real communion with Christ, they are also visible actions or signs through which men can have the image of what His life and death and resurrection means for them, and for the world, brought vividly before their minds.

We possess then, the image of God in the Church today, not in pictures or carvings or photographic reproductions, but in the Bible account of historical witnesses, in the preaching that repeats and sets forth their witness, and in the Sacraments. We must remember that the living Christ honours this image with His presence. As this image is presented to us in Word and Sacrament we are given not only what we call truth, but also what we call reality. We have not only something that points us to God, but God Himself in the midst, as He was in the midst in Jesus. God's purpose in giving us this image is not in order that we might have "some idea" of Him but in order that we might have fellowship with Him. The image is given to us in order to be God's meeting point with us for salvation and judgment.

5. The question of obedience

We all use aids to worship. Some use them in the form of statues and pictures accompanied by impressive traditional ritual and ceremony. Others invoke more "modern" means in films, effective lighting, touches of glamour softly accompanied by music. Some of our modern Protestant books of sermons are more crammed with illustrative modern imagery than the most ornate Churches of Roman Catholicism. Our teaching of the faith, in Sunday School, Bible Class, and theological Colleges would not be effective except against a background of images.

How far, in all this, do we violate or obey the Second Commandment? What images are we to use? Are we bound to try to re-present Jesus Christ as the image of God exactly and only as he appears in the pages of Holy Scripture? Or can we attempt to present Him in new ways and in new forms? Can we present a Christ clothed otherwise than as we find Him in the Bible? Or have we the right now to devise a new imagery in order to present Christ in a suitable modern form to the modern mind? Have we any reason to hope that God will use any or all the images or imagery we devise in order to help us to "put Christianity across" to the modern mind, or the "man in the street"?

In answering such questions we must above all remember that what ultimately matters in our worship within the Church, is not the numbers of people we can attract through our use of imagery, but simply the presence of God in the midst. What matters is whether or not our imagery really and faithfully points to the one real, true and living image which we have of God in Jesus Christ, as He presents Himself to us in Word and Sacrament. The dramatic, the powerful, the sensational, matter nothing here in comparison with the real. What matters alone is whether God Himself will honour with His Spirit and His presence the ways in which we seek to present Him.

There is a use of imagery which can violate the real purpose of the Second Commandment. Was it not meant to exclude anything that would obscure the clear presentation and reception of the image which Christ has left of Himself in Word and Sacrament? Many of us will believe that this image is best served by faithfulness in the exposition of Holy Scripture, and by a safeguarding of the simplicity and uniqueness of the sacraments. But whatever our own beliefs may be, the ultimate decision lies with God. "Them that honour me I will honour" was His word to Eli (1 Sam. 11.30). The ultimate question is: what kind of imagery will He honour with His gracious presence as we seek to set Him forth before men?

CHAPTER III

THE JEALOUSY THAT GUARDS GOD'S IMAGE

1. An imageless God?

THROUGHOUT the Old Testament we find a God who, from the human point of view, remained image-less. His voice was heard speaking clearly. His hand was often seen acting decisively within the human situation, but the image of what He is in Himself remained obscure and unrevealed. He gave Himself freely to His people in many different ways, but seemed to be jealous and sparing in giving any hints that would encourage His people to dare to try to paint a picture of Him or to carve a likeness of Him.

He was sparing even in the visions He gave to His people. Most often, in His approach to men, He spoke to them without giving them any vision at all. When Abraham was called out of Ur of the Chaldees in his first great encounter with the God of Israel we are not told that he saw God, but only that God spoke and said, "Get thee out" (Gen. xii.1). Abraham was dealing with One whom he knew must remain unimagined and unimaginable. When He drew near to Samuel and Eli in the Temple to make His will known and to call Israel back to Him, the only sign of His presence in the midst was that Samuel heard a voice speaking (1 Sam. iii). There was no visible form or appearance.

Certainly God did not deny His people the use of all visible symbols in their worship or thinking about Him. He occasionally allowed them the use of certain objects to stimulate their thought and devotion towards Himself. He allowed certain images to stand as signs of His presence, and allowed certain symbols to be used to stand for certain of His features. When He met Moses in the desert, He confronted Him not only through a voice, but also through the image of a bush which burned with fire and yet was not consumed (Ex. iii). When he led the children of Israel through the wilderness, He appeared to them in the image of a pillar of cloud by day and a pillar of fire by night. When He confronted the prophet Isaiah to make His will known, as well as speaking His word, He sealed it with a vision in which there was a magnificent representation of One seated on a throne high and lifted up and casting a huge train throughout the Jewish temple, surrounded by seraphim (Is. vi.1). He gave a like vision of Himself to the prophet Ezekiel. By such images, symbols and signs of His own choosing, He gave faint indications of what He was like. Yet these images, symbols and visions were so faint and enigmatic that, for His people, He remained the God who was known through His

Hindu: no image, word, n symbol man can
say of the ultimate is true. Brahma has no my
But what if He reveals Himself

voice and His mighty deeds rather than by His image. Even in the Temple, amongst the complicated ceremonies that men had to go through when they approached Him there, the only symbols of His presence were the Ark and the cherubim. Instead of an image of the merciful God who was to be worshipped and adored, there were only very faint signs of how superior He was to any possible man-made image or idea.

The people of God in the Old Testament, then, had to depend not so much on seeing forms or shapes, as on hearing God's voice and seeing His hand at work. They were taught that God was jealous lest they should even crave for images, or for any vivid likeness of Himself. They must be content with the voice which proclaimed His loving kindness. The psalmist is expressing something that lies at the heart of the faith and experience of the Old Testament when he utters the prayer, "Cause me to hear thy loving kindness" (Ps. cxliii.8). He desperately wants to experience God's fellowship and mercy. Yet he can hope to achieve this not by seeing God's face or even some faint outline or symbol, but simply by hearing the voice of One who speaks, and keeps His image hidden. "Take ye therefore good heed unto yourselves; for ye saw no manner of similitude on the day that the Lord spake unto you in Horeb out of the midst of the fire; lest ye corrupt yourselves and make you a graven image" (Deut. iv.15).

2. A people in tension and conflict

In this matter of His jealousy over His image tension often arose between God and His people, and conflict broke out.

Even the best servants of God felt at times a little frustrated and disappointed that God desired to remain so imageless, and gave them such little help in conceiving what He was like. Sometimes their encounters with Him left them in a state of disappointed suspense. Jacob after wrestling all through the dark night with the angel whom he believed to have the features of God, was forced to let go before the day broke and he could really see, and he had to be content to call this an experience of seeing God "face to face" (Gen. xxxii.24–30). Moses, later, having pleaded with God to let him see His glory,

was told that in response to his prayer he would be given a
vision of part of God's back (Ex. xxxiii.18–23).

But the ordinary people openly rebelled against not being
given a better "image" than they had for their God. The
conflict began immediately after the commandments were given,
when Moses disappeared up the mountain into the cloud for
forty days, and left them waiting. They found it a trial, after
the impressive religious ceremonies they had witnessed in
Egypt, to have been pledged now to serve a God who had
commanded their worship, devotion, and loyalty in a very
absolute way, and yet had tantalisingly given them no image
or picture or symbol of Himself on which they could now
centre that worship, devotion, and loyalty. "Make us something", they cried to Aaron, "to represent this terribly invisible
God! Give us an image that will make Him more real to our
senses and our minds!" No other nation on earth had to worship a purely invisible inconceivable God, as they were forced
to, for all the heathen deities around them had their various and
vivid symbols and images. Their hearts rebelled. We can understand them. We ourselves well know how affection can be kept
strong, and sometimes true, through even a photograph or a
ring or a lock of hair. They felt that God had not fully understood their religious cravings or catered adequately for their
religious needs. They forced an unwilling Aaron to make them
a golden calf to represent the "gods which had brought them
out of the land of Egypt" (Ex. xxxii.1–4).

All through their history, they were ready to take up the
same complaint, despising the images and symbols which God
had chosen to be the focus of His encounter with them at
worship, and craving for something more magnificent, and
naturally exciting. They were ashamed when they compared
the bareness of their temple with the imagery of the heathen
shrines. Where was their God? The conflict reached its climax
in the Northern half of the Kingdom under Jeroboam, after
the twelve tribes had split into two. King Jeroboam, ruling the
Northern tribes, felt that having set up a Kingdom to rival that
in the South, he must now set up a religious cult to rival that in
Jerusalem and to hold to the North the religious loyalty of his
people. So he built two Northern shrines in Samaria, one in

Bethel and one in Dan. This, in itself was a breaking of God's law which had commanded Israel to worship exclusively at the one temple at Jerusalem. But Jeroboam went much further. He knew well the natural craving in the people's heart for some imagery at the centre of their worship. He remembered their demands to Aaron, and in a deliberate violation of the Second Commandment he, too, had images made in the form of calves, to represent the Lord, and set them up, one at Dan and one at Bethel (1 Kings XII.28–30).

3. God's strange jealousy

At the very heart of this Second Commandment, "Thou shalt not make unto thee any graven image . . . thou shalt not bow down thyself to them," we are warned about the burning jealousy of God, and are threatened with fearful punishment if we ignore it, "for I the Lord thy God am a jealous God, visiting the iniquity of the fathers upon the third and fourth generation of them that hate me". Here we are up against God on an issue on which He will not, and cannot, change or compromise. Here He has set a careful watch, and uttered a special warning. Murder, adultery, theft, sabbath-breaking are all forbidden without such warning. This Commandment is specially singled out for it, and those who ignore this Commandment are called "them that hate me."

The details of the Old Testament story confirm this jealous and hopelessly unrelenting attitude of God over His decision on His image. We have seen how sparing He was in revealing any indication as to what an image of Him would be like. We have a further sign of His jealousy in the strange fierceness of the punishment which is described as coming upon Aaron and the people after their sin in this matter at Horeb. The same jealousy found expression in the stern denunciations by the prophets, of Jeroboam and his successors over the images in Dan and Bethel. They warned the people that their attendance at these shrines was going to bring a final and irrevocable doom on their nation. Their later historians tracing the reason why the Northern Kingdom of Israel deteriorated in its morale, and finally collapsed, had no hesitation in putting it down to these two images. Here, they believed, God's anger burns, and He indeed visits the iniquity of the fathers upon the children unto the third and fourth generation.

We may well wonder why God in this matter declares Himself so rigidly strict, and unrelenting. It is not usual for Him to frustrate the inventiveness and imagination of His people in this way. In most other aspects of His dealing with men He shows Himself yielding, willing to relent and to accommodate Himself to man's weaknesses and failures. We are forced, therefore, to call His attitude on the matter of His image "strange," and to give particular thought to the meaning of it.

4. The mercy that lies behind God's jealousy

One is often told the story of Michelangelo, in his work in Florence with the huge block of marble which other sculptors had rejected as too colossal and too awkward to be used for any purpose. He decided to work on it with a great and beautiful plan, but he did not communicate the final image to anyone, nor did he even allow onlookers to watch him as he chiselled out the statue. He erected a large shed over the block, and day after day, week after week he hid himself inside with his work, and those outside as they discussed what he was doing could only speculate a little impatiently as to what would ultimately be unveiled when the walls were removed. It was only when the work was completed that Florence was allowed to see the colossal statue of David, and understand what they had had to wait for.

Did Michelangelo conceal the image till the day of its unveiling, because, having something to say otherwise inexpressible until the work was unveiled, he wanted to avoid a false preliminary impression? If so, there is a slight analogy between what he did in Florence, and what God did in the Old Testament. The image of Himself in Jesus could not be understood by His people until the day of its final unveiling in Jesus. But throughout the history of Israel He was creating a true background against which it was to be interpreted and understood. He was at work rousing people's desire for it, making them expect something great, giving hints of its coming in sign and prophecy, promising it and yet still withholding it, till the final day of its revelation. It is in this light that we must interpret His strange jealousy. He is jealous to exclude every other image, because only through this one image can the truth be revealed.

The images that men could have themselves formed of God in Israel before Jesus came, were bound, in the light of His appearing, to have been proved only distortions of what God was going to reveal in Him. Therefore in the light of what He was going to do in truly revealing His image, God forbade any preliminary attempt to conjure it up in the human mind or to carve it in His temple. The image when it was finally revealed must be allowed to shine out clearly and purely against an uncorrupted background. God's jealousy over His final work refused to allow any background of false imagery to form in the life of Israel.

Moreover, God is jealous to exclude all man-made images of Himself, because He hates to be identified with our empty inventions, especially when it is a question of the centre of our human devotion and worship. He desires that the image we use in His name should always be filled with His real presence, and that our worship should involve real personal encounter with Himself. All through the Old Testament period He was seeking to bring in the day when He would reveal Himself to Israel in an image through which He would really communicate to men the fulness of His mercy and presence, an image that was Himself. This purpose was to be fulfilled in Jesus in whom men were to be given not just an image but also reality, not just truth but "spirit and truth," not just illumination but personal, face to face encounter, not just light but life also.

Therefore God jealously forbade worship through any man-made image in the Old Testament. Had they been able to choose images of God, even their best images would have been empty images which even if they could have offered a little light on the nature of God, and the stimulation of a little aesthetic beauty, would have offered no life, no encounter, no "spirit," no forgiving love and mercy. Men could have clung to and worshipped their empty image with its sublimity and beauty, and would have mistaken it for God. Surely it would

have been serious neglect of their welfare, if God had allowed
His people to toy with empty images, instead of waiting for the
true image through which He would mediate His presence and
His mercy for ever, and set up the true worship in Spirit and
in Truth.

It is the same love, then, that inspires God's dealings with
His people in both Testaments. Through the same love as
reveals the true image of Himself in Jesus, He has to withhold
his image in the Old Testament, and jealously guard it from
distortion. His jealousy, here is simply a form in which His
mercy meets us. Here He must exclude all the inventions of
human wisdom and imagination which could only destroy
what His love was aiming at. Here the human mind could have
produced only lies and emptiness, sublime lies perhaps, exciting
emptiness perhaps, but in the end, nothing but distortion and
vanity. It is therefore out of mercy that He makes men wait
with patience, understanding the struggle and agony of the
unfulfilled seeking that yearned after something more vivid and
real than in His hiddenness He could yet give them. But in the
fulness of time "The Word was made flesh and dwelt among us,
(And we beheld his glory, the glory as of the only begotten of the
Father,) full of grace and truth" (Jn. 1.14). "Blessed are your
eyes, for they see and your ears, for they hear," said Jesus.
"For verily I say unto you, that many prophets and righteous
men have desired to see those things which ye see, and have
not seen them, and to hear those things which ye hear, and
have not heard them" (Mt. xiii.16–17).

5. The conflict in the presence of Jesus

Even when confronted with the glory of the image of God
revealed fully in Jesus the human heart took offence, refused
to look and adore, complained, and craved for something
better.

Here was an image in flesh and blood, that is not only a
true likeness of God, but "God's presence and His very self."
"Here was One who pointed to Himself and to His work and
said, "He that hath seen me hath seen the Father" (Jn.
xiv.9). He lived and acted among men, giving the perfect

image of the love of God by laying His hand upon the leper in his uncleanness, and by stooping to identify Himself with the sinners whose company He always sought. He gave a perfect image of the holiness of God by condemning human sin in His words and in His own sinlessness, and by bearing it in agony as no other could ever do. He gave a perfect image of what some theologians call the transcendence of God, by remaining always Himself unique, kingly, separate even from those with whom He was completely identified. He gave a perfect image of the almightiness of God, in breaking the power of evil for ever through the weakness of the Cross, and in rising again in triumph over death.

It is true that when they were confronted by this image of God some responded with faith. They not only saw but also encountered God in Jesus. They received life and forgiveness from Him in Jesus and entered a continuing and growing fellowship with Him. "We beheld His glory" (Jn. 1.14). But such were simply extraordinary exceptions. "He was in the world, and the world was made by him, and the world knew him not. He came unto his own and his own received him not" (Jn. 1.10–11). The others refused to receive Him because they were offended at the image He presented to them. It was not impressive enough. It was an image given in too familiar terms. It was contrary to all that human wisdom and the best human tradition had taught them to expect.

The image God gave of Himself in Jesus was an image of wealth hidden in poverty, of majesty hidden in humility, of glory veiled in sin-bearing love, of righteousness hidden in mercy. It was the image of a king in the form of a suffering servant. It was the image of a God who comes into the midst of sinful men to seek and save them—a God who loves and stoops and identifies Himself with sinners. But man in his wisdom simply said, How impossible, and how stupid! Men in the presence of Jesus wanted something more divine and sublime. Was he not the carpenter's son from Nazareth? Did they not know his mother and his brothers? The sheer helplessness of His appearance at the very time when He made His most pointed kingly claims (Mk. xiv.62), was a final offence to the wisdom of His onlookers. How could their minds be expected ultimately to accept the fact that God in their midst would actually take the image of One dying on a Cross and crying with a loud voice, "My God, my God, why hast thou forsaken me?" (Mk. xv.34). Here again we have the old conflict between the hidden, loving God who cares for truth and for men, who cannot and will not deceive, and the impatient people who think themselves wiser than He, who measure by their own feelings, by their selfish demands and earthly standards, what He must do if He is to be God.

6. The continuing conflict today

Today within the Church, we to whom Jesus Christ presents Himself and His image through the Word of His apostles and the Sacraments of His Church, are faced with the same temptation to take offence over the lack of impressiveness and outward grandeur in what we are given to represent Him. How inadequate those "means of grace" seem, judged from an outward point of view, when we see them placed before us at the centre of our worship in the Church! A few words uttered in a sermon from a very ancient book about the man who was Himself an offence to the people of His time, a little bread, a little wine, a little water!

We too, at the very point where the image of God's mercy meets us in Jesus Christ, are tempted to become offended and thus to despise His wisdom, His self-revelation and self-offering, indeed His very presence. Because of the sheer simplicity and outward unimpressiveness of the image in which all this meets us and is mediated to us, we are tempted to pass it by, and to want another image than that which it pleases Him to give.

The Church in its history has often been quite frank in its attitude on this matter. It has regarded the Second Commandment as now having little application when it comes to the presentation of the image of God in Jesus Christ. Whereas in Old Testament times man had to restrain his craving for the visible imagery, it is argued, now in New Testament times, the danger which the Second Commandment was designed to avert is no longer a real threat, and everything the imagination of man can invent, and the hand of man fashion, can be used to make Him real to our generation today.

We know what the result of this way of thinking was in the Middle Ages. Pictures and statues of Jesus, portraying him in all the circumstances of His life, were brought into the centre of the worship of God and often made a focal point. Instead of being content with the Word and Sacraments which were left by Jesus to represent His image and be the means of His presence among men, other ceremonies were invented supplementing and elaborating the Church's ritual. All this was done with the best of intentions in an attempt to satisfy the craving of the people for the sensuous, and to add an attractive element regarded as absent from the simpler Gospel traditions.

The Reformation with its tendency to abolish the use of pictures and images as focal points of worship, and its return to the simplicity of the word and two sacraments instituted by Christ, was an attempt by the Church seriously to apply again the Second Commandment to its service of God. But today a fresh questioning has arisen about the validity of the Commandment. The Church has again grown anxious about its ability to attract, convince and hold the modern man with a worship that contains at its centre so little majestic movement, which tends to be void of colour or aesthetic value, and which appeals to the ear more than to the eye. The question which faced Aaron and Jeroboam in their day seems to face us. Have we any liberty to elaborate on what is already given by God to be the focal point of our worship of Himself? Is it legitimate to exercise our own powers of invention and imagination, and to be guided by our own wisdom and practical necessity, in this precise sphere?

In giving us the Second Commandment the purpose of God is to ensure the freedom of the images which He has Himself chosen for the service of His once-for-all revelation of Himself in Jesus Christ. The freedom that God wills for this image, and the grace that God wills to show to men, as they look towards Himself shown forth in it, tend to be endangered and spurned when humanly appointed images and ceremonies are allowed to stand alongside, or replace what God has given in His mercy.

"The whole history of Christendom" says Dale, "is a demonstration of the peril and ruin which came from any attempt to supplement by art and by stately and impressive rites, the revelation which God had made of Himself in Christ." We must remember that our man-made images and conceptions of God all tend to be nothing more or less than distortions of the truth as it has been revealed in the Word of God, and in the face of Jesus Christ. To be obedient in the presence and light of Jesus Christ means not only to looking at Him in order to learn everything we need to know about God from Him, but also to refuse to add to His image of God the contributions of our own wisdom and imaginations, which, in face of the real hidden glory of His image could only appear to be empty, ridiculous, and untrue. Here we have to bring our minds into obedience in acknowledging the sole glory of God. This obedience must be rendered not only in the sphere of theology, but also in the practices of our personal devotion and corporate worship.

It is well for us to remember today that the urgency behind this Commandment, with its fearful warnings, arises from the fact that what is at stake, in the question of our obedience or disobedience, is the presence of the gracious God in the midst. We must remember that it is easily and fatally possible for the Church to be relevant to the modern mind and yet be without God, popular without God, solemn and religious without the presence of God in the midst. What shall it profit a Church if it shall gain the whole world, and lose its own soul?

What matters, then, when a congregation gathers for worship, is not the amount of religious excitement we can create, or the pious devotion we can stimulate by a display of imagery either through eloquence in word, or skill in manipulation, or by the creation of "atmosphere" by music or colour. What matters is one simple fact, the presence of the merciful God in the midst through the Holy Spirit, as Jesus Christ incarnate, crucified and risen is set forth and offered to His people. But the presence of God Himself through the Holy Spirit to receive and inspire our worship is promised not to those who are most successful in the stimulation of such pious or religious atmosphere, but to those who seek Him simply through the symbols, images and ceremonies of His own choosing. No matter how difficult the situation may be for the Church in confronting the modern mind and the modern world, our policy in this matter must be decided not by anxiety but by faith in the Word of God.

THE THIRD COMMANDMENT

EXODUS XX.7. *Thou shalt not take the name of the Lord thy God in vain; for the Lord will not hold him guiltless that taketh his name in vain.*

CHAPTER IV

THE FREEDOM TO WORSHIP AND PRAY

1. God gives Himself a name

WE all believe, to some extent, in the value of knowing a person's name. The first task of anyone dealing with individuals within large groups, whether he is a pastor, or school-teacher, or welfare-worker, is to become familiar with the name of each one.

In the world in which the Gospel was enacted they believed even more realistically in the value of knowing the name of another. Every man, so it was thought, was bound to respond to his name. Therefore, to be able to call him by his name meant that you could more effectively claim his fellowship, help, and service. In the story of Jacob's wrestling with the angel, there came the stage when Jacob, with his thigh put out of joint in the struggle, hung helpless in the arms of his divine visitor from beyond, by whom he still wanted to be blessed. But in his weakness the thought came, "Even though I am beaten, if only I knew his name I might have a real power to prevail with him in another way." So he began to cling to the stranger with his weakness, and he cried out "Tell me, I pray thee, thy name." He was certain that the knowledge of this heavenly stranger's name would enable him in the future to deal with him on a more equal and satisfying basis (Gen. XXXII.29).

In the heathen world around Israel, this belief in the power of a name was degraded often to a sheer superstition. The devotees of the heathen cults felt that the mere use of the name of their god had some virtue in itself. When, for example, Elijah challenged the priests of Baal to prove the power of their god on Mount Carmel, they leaped on their altar, cut themselves with knives and called on the name of Baal incessantly from morning till noon, "O Baal hear us," in the belief that the mere repetition of his name could compel their god to

work a miracle (1 Kings xviii.26). When Jesus, in the midst of
a similar heathen environment, was confronted in the region of
Gadara by one possessed by devils, in the course of His efforts
to heal the man He asked the devils what their name was, and
received the reply "My name is Legion: for we are many"
(Mk. v.9). One of the simplest explanations of this question is
that Jesus well knew the common superstition, that the name
of an evil spirit gave you power to command it, and He was not
ashamed, for the purposes of His love, to play the part of the
ordinary healers who practised such methods.

In the midst of a world like this, where men believed that a
name could be used in such a way, the true and eternal God
gave Himself a name. The Second Commandment reminded
us that God, though invisible, has descended to the level of
what is visible, has expressed Himself in an image, and identified Himself with this image. Now in this Commandment we
are reminded that, with all His glory and namelessness, He has
descended also to take a place in this world's life as a god who
can be named with a personal name, alongside a multitude of
other so-called "gods." God in coming into the midst of our
human life has come not only into the world of our images but
also into the midst of our use and abuse of names. Before the
people whose worship and service He seeks, He has taken upon
Himself a name for which He has promised to listen so that He
can respond to it, a name to which He has promised to respond
in faithfulness and truth, and which He has trusted them to
honour and use with reverence and fear. The particular name
for Himself which He chose to give to His people in the Old
Testament was the Hebrew name which spells out letters
usually transcribed "Yahweh." This Hebrew name has been
translated in our authorised version by the term, "the Lord,"
though many people in the past have thought, erroneously, that
the Hebrew letters for this name should be written out to spell
in English: "Jehovah." However we try to translate those
letters today, it was by this name that God, in His grace and
love, willed to be known, worshipped, discussed, and preached
about in the midst of the life of His people. Throughout the
centuries God was never ashamed to identify Himself with all
that the name of Yahweh came to mean for the people of Israel.

God gave Himself this name not in order that His people might have power over Him, or have Him at their disposal, as the heathen imagined they had their gods, but in order to enable them with real freedom to call on His help in their need and to enter a worshipful and uplifting fellowship with Himself. God gave them His name in order that they might have freedom to approach Him, invoke and worship Him, believing that in His own freedom and love He would come into their midst to receive their worship and to give them His personal fellowship. God gave them His name in order that they might use it boldly and freely, regularly and reverently.

Such is the grace of God even in the Old Testament. But in the New Testament there is something indeed new, something even more wonderful. Here God identifies Himself with a man who has the name of Jesus of Nazareth, and the name Yahweh is needed no more.

And in this new name we have His true name. A name, if it is to be true and not false, must express as far as possible the character of its owner. Time and again in the Bible we find men being given names that express the kind of men they are. Therefore to know the true name of God we must come to know what the name of Jesus Christ means. We must enter His friendship and experience the forgiveness and strength that His companionship and word can give us. When we know what this name means and stands for, we indeed know who God is. God's name is now, "The God and Father of our Lord Jesus Christ." The world had to wait till the first Christmas when Jesus was born at Bethlehem in order to know this true name of the eternal God. "Thou shalt call His name Jesus, for He shall save His people from their sins" (Mt. 1.21). In Him God has given Himself a name to which He has bound Himself for ever. The name of Jesus is now the true address of God.

2. The promises given with the name

(i) The taking of oaths

In the Old Testament, the name of Yahweh was given to be used by men in order to help them to find a greater and more stable source of inspiration and strength for their enterprises than could be found in any appeal to their own integrity or strength. The tasks to which men were called to pledge themselves in the service of Yahweh were such that mere human resolution would have failed to bring about their accomplishment. In order to obtain the stability and fortitude required for all such tasks, men, knowing their own frailty were encouraged to bind themselves to fulfil them through vows taken in the name of Yahweh, and before His presence. Through the taking of such oaths they were assured of the strength that is promised to all who call upon God's name. They were thus lifted into a sphere of new possibilities. "Thou shalt fear the Lord thy God, and shalt serve him, and shalt swear by his name" (Deut. VI.13). When Ruth pledged herself to follow God's call to her to identify herself with Naomi and her people, and to be faithful in the midst of all the sufferings that such a call involved, it was undoubtedly with a sense of her own inadequacy that she added the binding oath: "The Lord do so to me, and more also, if ought but death part thee and me" (Ruth I.16–17). Through the power of the name of Yahweh a man can now "swear to his own hurt" and be held to the course to which he has pledged himself (Ps.xv.4). An extreme illustration of this is given in the grim story of Jephthah's daughter (Judges XI).

Moreover, since human witness so often contains inaccuracy and falsehood, God allowed the use of His name to attest the truth of human witness, and thus to become the inspiration of a new desire and effort after truth. A man's word, given under such an oath, was to be taken so seriously that even where there was no corroborative evidence to support it, trust was placed in it (Ex. XXII.10–11). The action of a community in allowing oaths to be sworn in their courts, not simply in the name of loyalty to the community and its principles, but in the name of God, is an acknowledgment that the community recognises the weakness that is inherent in mere humanly based words and pledges. Such human weakness is being overcome when men are allowed to swear in the name of One who has proved Himself to be the source of a greater faithfulness and truth in human life.

(ii) *The invocation of God's presence*

The gift of the name of God to Israel meant His presence in the midst of the life and worship of Israel.

When He called the Prophets, and commanded them to speak to Israel words "in His name," they fulfilled His command believing that, as they spoke, the Lord Himself would be with them in the midst, and would give power and authority to their utterance, making their words effective in bringing the blessing and destiny His Word promised. To speak in the name of the Lord implied the gift of His presence with the speaker.

They believed also that the gift of the name of Yahweh meant His presence in the midst of their worship and rejoicing. To help them to use His name regularly, boldly, and freely, Yahweh had appointed for them special ceremonies and feasts to which He wanted to be invited. He chose also special places at which they were to celebrate the ceremonies, sacrifices, and feasts connected with His name. Several times in the book of Deuteronomy, for example, God's presence is promised at the place of His name. "There shall be a place which the Lord your God shall choose, to cause his name to dwell there; thither shall ye bring all that I command you . . . and all your choice vows which ye vow unto the Lord; and ye shall rejoice before the Lord your God" (Deut. XII.11–12; XIV.23–24). In instituting all this detailed and carefully defined ritual of the Old Testament, God was concerned to become their guest and thus to bring His people into fellowship with Himself. "An altar of earth shalt thou make unto me. . . . In all places where I record my name I will come unto thee and bless thee" (Ex. XX.24).

But, above all, God's gift of His name to Israel meant that He wanted to be invited into their presence through prayer, both in the ordinary routine of their lives, and at the time of their direst need. The knowledge of His name and all that it implied meant that they could now pray to Him with confidence. "The name of the Lord is a strong tower," says the proverb: "the righteous runneth into it and is safe" (Prov. XVIII.10). This meant that in all the dangers of life, wherever a man might be, he needed neither altar nor temple nor fortress, but could immediately find help and defence in calling on the name of the Lord in prayer from the situation in which he found himself. The psalmist echoes the same thought in his word of benediction, "The name of the God of Jacob defend thee" (Ps. xx.1). They could actually rate the knowledge of the name of Yahweh as a more important factor in national defence than their traditional armaments. "Some trust in chariots and some in horses, but we will remember the name of the Lord our God" (Ps. xx.7).

In the New Testament the name of Jesus Christ is substituted for the name of Yahweh at the centre of a multitude of such promises of blessing and help, and affirmations of faith. The Apostles used it boldly and freely in their preaching, recalling all that Jesus had meant and done, proclaiming through Him forgiveness and victory. As they did so the risen and exalted Lord honoured their word and gave such power to the preaching of His name that the Kingdom of God was constantly advanced, men were healed, devils were cast out, and the Church increased in its power to witness and suffer. But Jesus had not only given them a word to speak in His name, He had also given them the Lord's Supper and Baptism to celebrate in His name in the midst of their fellowship, with special assurance of His presence as they celebrated these. On such occasions they gathered "in His name" looking to Him in simple and true faith, and claiming His promise "where two or three are gathered together in my name, there am I in the midst of them" (Mt. xviii.20). They were certain as they did so, that He came to them and blessed them and their actions, and sealed what they did with His own activity and power.

Moreover they used the name of Jesus to invoke His presence in all the varied situations of everyday life. They remembered that He had gone to the home of Jairus when his little daughter had been critically ill, and had accepted the invitation to be the guest at the wedding at the home in Cana of Galilee. He was still the same Jesus "today and for ever" (Heb. xiii.8), and would accept the invitation to come to every Christian home in order to share in such sorrows and joys. They therefore called upon the name of Jesus with confidence that it had no less power and authority than the name of Yahweh in Old

Testament times. Had he not promised, "whatsoever ye shall ask in my name, that will I do, that the Father may be glorified in the Son. If ye shall ask anything in my name, I will do it" (Jn. xiv.13–14)? Of this they were certain: "that at the name of Jesus every knee should bow, of things in heaven and things in the earth and things under the earth: And every tongue should confess that Jesus Christ is Lord, to the glory of God the Father" (Phil. ii.10–11).

It is in this context and at this point that we begin to encounter most powerfully the challenge of this commandment for our personal and Church life today. If we know the name of Jesus and all that it stands for, we know the true name of God, the name that He cannot and will not deny, for He has for ever identified Himself with it. Knowing this name we know the secret of God's heart, we know that which gives us power and status before Him, and fills our life with all kinds of new possibilities. Now we need no longer be afraid to speak to God and to come to Him for daily forgiveness. Now, with the knowledge of this name, we will have something to say for ourselves even in the hour when our sins finally accuse us, and we are tormented by thoughts of judgment. Now, in knowing this name, we know that by which we can cast out the devils first from our own heart and life, and then from this distracted and possessed world in which we live. Now we have a purpose to live for, and a message for all our fellow men that can turn their darkness into light indeed.

3. The warnings given with the name

"Ye shall not swear by my name falsely, neither shalt thou profane the name of thy God: I am the Lord" (Lev. xix.12). New and dreadful possibilities in profanity and perjury are brought near to those who know the name of the Lord. For an individual to take the giving of an oath lightly is so serious that the commandment contains the special warning: "the Lord will not hold him guiltless that taketh his name in vain". It is an equally serious sin for a community to allow oaths to be lightly taken, or to extort oaths from its members, binding them to any unworthy purpose, or seeking to harness their devotion and loyalty to any ends that do not further God's kingdom.

The taking of oaths, at the time of Jesus, had become the occasion and cause of widespread insincerity of speech. If oaths were so important, men argued, then when no oath was taken a man's word need not be trustworthy in itself. Moreover, in order to find a way to avoid the urgency of keeping vows given under oath, men began to swear not directly by the name of God, but by objects associated with God, such as heaven or the temple or the altar. It was in reaction to such insincerity that some well known teachers and sects, such as the Essenes, forbade altogether the taking of oaths, and Jesus Himself, in the light of the imminence of His Kingdom and of God's judgment-seat, spoke a final warning about all such insincerity: "Ye have heard that it hath been said by them of old time, Thou shalt not forswear thyself, but shalt perform unto the Lord thine oaths: but I say unto you, Swear not at all; neither by heaven; for it is God's throne: nor by the earth; for it is his footstool: neither by Jerusalem; for it is the city of the great King. . . . But let your communication be, Yea, yea; Nay, nay: for whatsoever is more than these cometh of evil" (Mt. v.33–37). These words are meant to recall men to the purpose for which the authority of the name of God was given to their oaths. Instead of such oaths being made a pretext and excuse for insincerity in ordinary speech, they were meant to be the starting point of a new effort after faithfulness and truth in ordinary words and promises. Now that Jesus Himself has brought His Kingdom into the midst of this world's life, the same seriousness that once marked the taking of oaths in the name of the Lord, must now mark all our everyday affirmations and negations. In all this our behaviour will be a sign as to whether we belong to the Kingdom of God or to the kingdom of the evil one.

Throughout Old Testament times the third commandment stood as a warning to men not simply in the taking of oaths, but also in all their exercises of worship and prayer, and in their service of the Word of God. As this Commandment was handed down from generation to generation, it was accompanied by stories of how the most severe and deadly punish-

ment came upon men who profaned the service of the altar and
temple, thus profaning the name of the Lord. In later days even
when they read the Scripture, pious Jews became afraid even
to pronounce the sacred name "Yahweh," and substituted for
it some other divine name, the careless use of which would not
involve them in such guilt and danger.

Their fear arose from their belief that God hated His name
to be used without faith, or without a true discernment of what
it meant to call on Him and to invoke His presence or His
authority. Jeremiah in his day pronounced stern condemnation on the prophets who spoke in the name of Yahweh without
true understanding, and uttered the "dreams" and imaginations of their own heart instead of His word (Jer. xiv.15; xxiii.
25). And we find the other prophets frequently expressing their
abhorrence of the use of God's name in the Temple by a people
whose lives and manner of worship showed no sign of real
living faith in Him. Such a show of piety and enthusiasm, no
matter how dignified, solemn, correct, and orderly, was a
taking of His name in vain and an abomination in His sight.
"To what purpose is the multitude of your sacrifices unto me?
saith the Lord: I am full of the burnt offerings of rams, and the
fat of fed beasts; and I delight not in the blood of bullocks and
of goats, and the fat of fed beasts or lambs or of he goats. When
ye come to appear before me, who hath required this at your
hand, to tread my courts? Bring no more vain oblations;
incense is an abomination unto me; the new moons and the
sabbaths and the calling of assemblies, I cannot away with;
it is iniquity, even the solemn meeting" (Is. 1.11–13).

4. Our abuse and neglect of the name

In every aspect of our Church life today we are in danger
of taking the name of the Lord in vain. Even in the offering of
our praise we can either maintain a cold dignity in which
there is no sacrifice of the heart, or put on the artificial fervour
that arises from the singing of a catchy tune that has no relation
either to the Word which God has spoken to us, or the words
that we must speak to Him. In our preaching we can give
utterance "in the name of the Father, the Son and of the Holy

Ghost" to what is merely a string of chatty anecdotes and pop illustrations, with no attempt to set forth the name of the Holy Trinity, to proclaim which has been the whole purpose of our calling to the ministry. And in our listening we can slouch back in our pews and eat confectionary as if the House of God were a cheap place of amusement. We can administer baptism to infants as if it were simply a way of assuring that the growing life of a community shall have some flavour of traditional Christianity about it, and in the process we can use the name of Jesus to extract vows, the implications of which are only vaguely understood. We can find ourselves praying without really desiring half the things we pray for, and then ending up with the usual formula, "in the name of Jesus Christ." We can make the Lord's Supper an occasion for "checking in" our annual Church attendance. We can talk piously about Christian stewardship of talents and time, and yet all the time be concerned chiefly with the financial aspect.

At the time of the Reformation, it was with this Third Commandment in mind that the Reformers sought to criticise and correct the abuses they found in the Roman Church. Throughout its history the Church has always been tempted to make the simple rites of the Lord's Supper and Baptism to which Jesus especially attached His name much more elaborate than the Word of God warrants. The abuses which cluttered up the Roman Church in the middle ages, were mainly due to such deliberate invention of new and more elaborate ceremonies and forms of worship, all in the name of Jesus, and yet without any authority from Him. The protest of the Reformers was against men trying to be wiser than God in these matters, and their aim in reform was to restore within the Church only those ceremonies in which they had clear authority from Jesus to use His name, and thus to expect His presence. We in our day are tempted to wonder if the preaching of the Word and the administration of the Sacraments in the name of Jesus really constitute a sufficiently vivid and attractive ritual to have at the heart of a Church, which has to hold the loyalty and love of modern men and women. Our temptation is to try something new, something more modern, exciting, and dramatic, in the name of Jesus, in order to meet the demands of the modern mind which we find so unusually difficult to please. Here we must face a most important question: Have we any authority to make such elaborations and inventions "in the name of Jesus"? And if we have not, dare we solemnly and authoritatively invoke His presence through His name, as we perform our self-appointed ritual? Is this not a perverse abuse of the gift of His name from which the Commandment is there to save us?

But surely even worse than the perverse abuse of the name of Jesus is our sloth and neglect in face of the gift of the name of Jesus, and the challenge it gives us. His name is given us to be used and to be witnessed to, but we act as if we had never heard of it. "Hitherto ye have asked nothing in my name: ask and ye shall receive" (Jn. XVI.24), was His challenge to His disciples. It is still true that many of us "ask nothing." Nor can our neglect of the ordinance of Baptism escape judgment in this connection. It is quite clear, for instance, that in New Testament times Baptism in the name of Jesus was a source of strength to the early Christians in the struggle they had in living the Christian life. It brought home to them vividly the reality of Christ's once-for-all forgiveness, and of His promise never to fail them at any stage in this life. It related them in a living way through the Spirit to the power of Christ's death and resurrection. But how few of us ever try to "improve our Baptism" by thinking about it, and asking seriously what Christ has to say to us and to give us through it from day to day! Moreoever, if we have serious questions to ask about our use of Baptism, we must also ask if four celebrations of the Lord's Supper in a year is a sufficient response on our part in the use of this gracious means of ever-renewed communion with Himself, by which we are meant to grow in grace and in the knowledge of Himself.

5. The challenge to our faith

All these outward forms of the abuse, perversion, and neglect of the name of Jesus Christ arise from an unhealthy attitude of mind and heart which today prevails generally within the Church, breaking out in many different directions and revealing itself in varied symptoms. We must not therefore single out for special condemnation any one of these aspects of the problem that have already been listed—especially when we on our own part are bound to be guilty of the same thing in some different form. Certainly we must not condemn too loudly the "swearing" and the perjury that sometimes take place in the world around us, if we have not first put the house of God in order. Judgment must begin here. Basically this unhealthy attitude arises out of a sheer lack of faith that the name of Christ means the presence of Christ. Without such faith "it is impossible to please God" (Heb. xi.6).

The danger we are in through allowing such an attitude to prevail cannot be overstressed. We tend to drift easily in a downward spiral. Lack of faith is forced to take the form of habitual insincerity. Insincerity in its turn breeds unreality, and this gives rise ultimately to a mockery that must result in what Paul calls "damnation." Paul found such a state of affairs arising in Corinth, and he wrote to warn them that at their Lord's table, "he that eateth and drinketh unworthily, eateth and drinketh damnation to himself, not discerning the Lord's body," adding further strange words: "for this cause many are weak and sickly among you, and many sleep" (1 Cor. xi.29–30). We must remember that the name of Jesus Christ in the midst of His Church, even on perverse and insincere lips, is more powerful than the sin of the man who uses it. As His name is used, as the Word is read and preached, as the Sacraments are administered, He fulfils in His grace the promise of His presence. But it is a fearful thing for God to be present in the face of the sheer human insincerity that has arisen out of long continued faithlessness.

Yet it is no cure to run away from the grace of God in order to try to avoid abusing it. In this way we only incur the damnation of neglecting God's grace. To whom shall we go, if not to Him who says "Thou shalt not take the name of the Lord thy God in vain"? The abuse of oaths current in His day did not prevent our Lord either from swearing when He Himself was put on oath (Mt. xxvi.63–4) or from using in His ordinary speech phrases which can be interpreted as oaths (e.g. Mk. viii, 12). Our only refuge from the judgment threatened in this commandment is in the far greater and more important promise on which its warning is based. If we turn to Him in penitence and faith we shall never take His name in vain. The Word of God with its promises will become to us indeed the word of pardon, cleansing and new life. The Sacraments will indeed become a renewed means of encounter with our reigning and forgiving Lord. The help we seek will come. The light we need will shine in our darkness. The enemies we must overcome will vanish before us. And with this name on our lips, and faith in it in our hearts, we will be assured that nothing can henceforth separate us from His love and power.

THE FOURTH COMMANDMENT

EXODUS XX.8–11. *Remember the Sabbath day, to keep it holy. Six days shalt thou labour, and do all thy work: but the seventh day is the sabbath of the Lord thy God: in it thou shalt not do any work, thou, nor thy servant nor thy maidservant, nor thy cattle, nor the stranger that is within thy gates. For in six days the Lord made heaven and earth, the sea, and all that in them is, and rested the seventh day: wherefore the Lord blessed the sabbath day, and hallowed it.*

CHAPTER V

THE MEANING OF THE SABBATH

1. God and His Sabbath

"IN six days the Lord made heaven and earth, the sea, and all that in them is." In the first two chapters of the book of Genesis we are shown God at work, and thus given a picture of how every true workman should go about His work. In His work in creation, God lavishes boundless skill, energy and inventiveness. The writer rejoices in recording the details of every fresh outpouring of His creative love and imagination. Everything is done according to a plan and purpose that neglects not even the smallest detail, and yet everything is the product of a free and spontaneous enthusiasm. Perhaps Jesus had these early chapters of Genesis in mind when He said "My Father worketh hitherto, and I work" (Jn. v.17), comparing what He found there with the intense, concentrated, tireless energy which He Himself put into His own ministry.

But the Lord whose activity is described in the first two chapters of Genesis does not absorb Himself without any reserve in the work of creation. In the midst of all this lavish and hard activity, God Himself remains detached from the work He is doing. After each day's work He pauses, stands back, collects Himself again, looks with careful judgment on what He has accomplished, and pronounces it "good." And on the seventh day, after He has completed all things, and made man, we read that "God ended his work which he had made: and he rested on the seventh day from all his work which he had made" (Gen. ii.2). This picture of God pausing and resting from His work, reminds us that God has given only a limited amount of Himself to the task of making and upholding the heaven and the earth. God is free from what He has made. He has kept His real self apart from creation in such a way as to be able to look upon His creatures, rejoice over them, and relate Himself in complete freedom to them in a new and fresh way, a way to which He had not yet given expression in His creative activity. That "the Lord rested the seventh day" means that He has not allowed the activity of the days of creation to exhaust him or bind Him, and has limited creation purposely. He has something to say that could not be said in the work of the six days, something to give that is not yet given through all the enthusiasm and wealth He has put into this world in creating it.

What God has kept back from creation is here described in terms of a Sabbath rest. "In six days the Lord made heaven and earth . . . and rested the seventh day: wherefore the Lord blessed the sabbath day and hallowed it." What God has reserved in Himself, in limiting His creative work and taking this Sabbath rest, is much more wonderful than He has already given to creation through His work. After all, six days are only six days, but the Sabbath rest is eternal! God, has therefore something new and something extra to give this world over and above what He has already given to it in its creation. The fact that He wants to share this also with man is made clear by the fact that He not only gives Himself a Sabbath day, but gives one to man too, and "blesses" it to man's use. In and through it, He is going to make a new approach to man in order to give to man what He has reserved within Himself over and above creation.

2. Man and the Sabbath

The thought expressed in the latter half of the commandment, which is a quotation from the account of creation given in the second chapter of Genesis, is that "God blessed the Sabbath day and hallowed it" in order that on each Sabbath day of his life on earth, man himself might be led to lift his heart above this creation and apart from this creation, above and apart from his daily work and leisure and sport, in order to share in the Sabbath rest which God has reserved in Himself above and apart from this created world.

"The Sabbath was made for man" (Mk. 11.27), Jesus said. It is significant that in the account which we have of creation,

God did not finally take or seek to express His Sabbath rest till He had completed the making of man. Up till that point He only paused, but in the making of man God has achieved the creature who can really grasp, receive, and live by that which He wants to express and give through the Sabbath. Man is made to share in the freedom from toil within the created world, and in the rejoicing over it, which God indulged in, in taking His Sabbath rest. He is made to respond freely to the new and personal approach of love, which God reserved as His Sabbath activity towards this world. And in this way man is made in the image of God Himself. Therefore when He has completed the work of making man, God can really give expression to His Sabbath rest within creation.

This, then, is the deep and wonderful mystery which lies at the heart of the institution of the Jewish Sabbath day. It is as if God said: "I will put a Sabbath day at the heart of the order of things in this universe, and I will bless this Sabbath day weekly as it comes round, and on this day I will communicate to man My own Sabbath rest. On this day I will truly share with him that in Myself which I have kept back so far from creation. On this day I will come near as the God of rest, joy, and freedom, whose delight it is to give rest, joy, and freedom before Myself." God gave the Sabbath to the men of the Old Testament because He wanted them through it to share that in Himself which they could find neither through His own work in creation, nor through their own daily work in the midst of creation. On this day His purpose is that they should lift up their eyes and their hearts above His work in the created world in order to have the fellowship with Himself, which He is there freely to give as His gift to men who have ceased from their works. In this way he seeks to share with men the best part of Himself which He has kept back from creation. Right through the Old Testament God, on each Sabbath, is saying to His people, "Come unto me all ye that labour and are heavy laden and I will give you rest."

The Sabbath day, then, stands not only for something that is eternally reserved in the heart of God, but also for something in the heart of God which He wants to share with man here and now. It is therefore not to be thought of as primarily a social institution arising out of necessary natural, cultural, psychological, or physical grounds. It was given to the Jews in order that they might be saved from missing the meaning of life by becoming completely absorbed in the work of this world, and thus losing themselves. It was given to save them from the vain effort of trying to find the source of true fellowship with God within the ordinary framework of the created world. It was given to prevent them from mistaking for God Himself, what they found within nature or within themselves, or through their own efforts in work or culture, even their best efforts. On each Sabbath, as it arrived, they were to lay down their tools, desist from their sport and culture and their own self expression, relax, and listen to the Word of God as it said, "Listen to Me as I draw near to speak, and respond to Me as I draw near to offer you my fellowship, and seek this day to draw you to Myself. Cease from your absorption in creation and look up and take from Me that which cannot be found in the routine and rhythm of earthly life with its toil and rest, its work and play." Through the Sabbath, and what He commands on the Sabbath, God wants to put His Sabbath rest in man's heart. This is the primary reason for the commandment, as it is given here. It is intended not simply that man should relax but that he might find rest, freedom, and joy before God and in this creation through the blessing which God has specially attached to this day, and promised to those who seek it and keep it in faith.

As man in the Old Testament shared with God in the blessing of the Sabbath, he was enabled to find the true meaning not only of his own relationship to God but also of his earthly work and his future destiny. The gift of the Sabbath reminded him that he was not made for his work. In the account of its institution, it is clearly in the author's mind to show us that before man is even sent out to begin his work, he is first called on to enter the freedom and joy of the full fellowship God offers in the Sabbath—quite apart from any consideration as to whether he has worked hard or not so hard. Work here is the outflow of what he finds in the Sabbath. The Sabbath is the real thing. Moreover, in the midst of his career of work in this world, he has to allow his progress in building and striving and struggling during the week to be constantly interrupted and even hindered, by the breaking in of the Sabbath. In the midst of his career of work, he is called on, through being forced regularly to turn away from it, to give a sign that he knows he cannot find the meaning of existence through the daily activity that has absorbed so much of his energy. Indeed, through the interruption of the Sabbath, he is forced to confess that he finds the meaning of his destiny, his life and work, in release from his work rather than in the midst of his work.

Certainly for man in the Bible work must be regarded as an infinitely serious and significant part of his life and task. This aspect of daily work is stressed all the more since, according to the Bible, man is a fallen being, out of harmony with his environment, having to earn his bread in the sweat of his brow and fight for existence against natural forces that seem to have turned against him. This requires very serious work indeed. Certainly, too, by the grace of God, this daily work has a positive meaning and purpose, and a rich meaning at that. Man's labour is "not in vain" (cp. Ps. CIV.23; 1 Cor. xv.58). But it is only through the Sabbath that man finds out that daily labour has true meaning; and it is only through what is given him in the Sabbath that he finds the strength and vision necessary for him to carry on the struggle victoriously. The Kingdom to which his work must be consecrated will come in response to the faith that waits on God and works in glad expectancy, rather than to the zeal that toils in hope of the fruit of its own efforts. No matter how serious and absorbing his daily work, he must always resist the temptation to regard this as his main activity and the Sabbath as a secondary period of relaxation, designed to make him more fit for this activity. It is the Sabbath that must always be served by, and allowed to cast its light on, everything else he does.

The Sabbath was given to man, not only to make him look up to God above the world, but also to make him look forward as he looks up. The Jews were taught by their Prophets that the great event of their future would be the reign of a Messiah upon the earth when creation was renewed and the Kingdom of God finally established. The Sabbath day was regarded as a sign given by God that their new age would indeed come as

God's gift from beyond, breaking into time as the Sabbath day broke into their work and their week. The peace, rest, liberty, and joy of their Sabbaths were regarded as a foretaste of the greater, more secure and lasting liberty, peace, and joy which would be given for ever to their nation and to the world when the age of the Messiah or the Kingdom of God, dawned upon the earth. Viewed in this light, the Sabbath was indeed a sign and foretaste of the Kingdom of God.

We can illustrate what this aspect of the gift of the Sabbath could mean to a pious Jew whose life during the week was full of poverty and struggle, in a very simple story. Suppose a man lives in the heart of a great city at a time of poverty and distress when he finds it hard even to earn a living, and has not the faintest hope of enjoying any luxury as the fruit of his labour. One day he receives a letter from lawyers in a distant land, telling him that he is now the heir of a great fortune. But he cannot have his inheritance for many years to come. As a relief in his plight, however, they have arranged that regularly for one day in the week he will be able to live like a prince with credit given him in every expensive eating place and every place of rich entertainment he might wish to go to. To remind him that he is the heir to untold wealth, he can live like a prince for one day out of seven. For six days it is to be hard labour, monotonous toil, plain and mundane living. But what a difference the one day in the week makes to him, the day in which the pledge of his great and future status arrives and he can don his different clothes and go out and live like a prince!

As the Jew found this meaning in the Sabbath, his daily work took on a new light. He was not simply enabled to endure its hardness bravely, but he was enabled to see that in a strange way his daily work, too, was geared to the purpose for which the Sabbath was given to him. He discovered this, however, not through any hidden goodness inherent in his daily work, but simply by seeing it in the light which the Sabbath day cast upon it—and always he lived, not so that the Sabbath rest might serve the other six days, but so that the other six days might serve the Sabbath rest.

3. Christ and the Sabbath

If we wish to define more exactly than we have done, what it was that God sought to share with the Jews through the gift of the Sabbath in the Old Testament, we need only look at Jesus Christ. Everything that God held out to the Jews in blessing the Sabbath day to them, is held out to us in a new and better way in Christ. In Jesus, present among men in Galilee and Jerusalem, offering them His friendship, God Himself was present amongst men in a renewed call to them to enter the fellowship of His Sabbath rest, liberty, and joy. The risen Christ present in the midst of the Church today, as it gathers for worship, for the hearing of the Word, and for the celebration of the Lord's Supper, is to us today what the Sabbath Day in the midst of the week was to the Jew.

A great deal of Jesus' teaching and activity can be understood in the light of this fact. "Come unto me, all ye that labour and are heavy laden, and I will give you rest" He said (Mt. xi.28). In this call He re-echoes what God said to his people on every Sabbath day from the earliest times of their national history. It is a call to share freely, here and now, through His own friendship, the perfect and eternal joy and rest which it was in God's heart to give to man in the beginning, when He created him good, and destined him as the companion of His glory. Jesus was conscious that He had come to impart precisely this blessing to men. And when He added, "take my yoke upon you, and learn of me; . . . for my yoke is easy, and my burden is light" (Mt. xi.29–30), He promised men that through participation in this Sabbath rest, they would go forth with a new attitude to the tasks imposed on them by life in this world, having now been made free from bondage of heart and mind to the labour of the weekday.

On at least three occasions Jesus expressed in very deliberate actions, His claim to be the One who had come to fulfil the promise to men given originally in the Sabbath day. When He saw a woman in the Synagogue whose posture was dreadfully distorted by disease, He cured her, saying, "Ought not this woman . . . whom Satan hath bound, lo, these eighteen years be loosed from this bond on the Sabbath day?" (Lk. xiii.16).

Two things are clear in Jesus' mind. Firstly, the Sabbath is
the day above all other days for men and women to come into
their own inheritance of freedom before God, a freedom that is
His gift apart from all considerations of work or human effort.
And, secondly, He, Himself, is the one who has come in God's
name to bring this freedom to a world that has fallen into
bondage by failing to claim it. In defending His disciples
against the criticisms of the Pharisees when they winnowed
corn in the fields with their hands, and thus broke the strict
requirements of the Jewish legislation on the Sabbath, Jesus
not only called Himself "Lord of the Sabbath" but also referred
to an action of King David and His followers in eating the
priests' shewbread in the temple on a Sabbath when they were
hungry. The implication was that, with David's example,
before Him, He Himself as the Messiah whom David fore-
shadowed, has the right at least to pattern His Sabbath activity
on that of His great forebear. He has come to bring liberty and
joy to the world, and He must give signs in His ministry that
this is in truth the original promise that God made to mankind
through the gift of the Sabbath day. Man must now be free on
the Sabbath to look up and enter a glad, free, confident, and
restful relationship with His heavenly Father.

Jesus' resurrection, however, is the clearest sign of all that
He has come to bring into the midst of the world's life in a new
way the true reality of the gift of which the Sabbath was a sign.
When the risen Christ came into the midst of the disciples
during the forty days after Easter, they knew they were in the
presence of the eternal Kingdom of God, that the New Age
had broken into the midst of this present world with power
even over death. When He breathed on them, giving them
His spirit, and communicating to them His peace, joy, and
liberty, they knew that this was indeed what God intended
to breathe into this world's life in blessing the Sabbath day and
hallowing it. Here was the inheritance of which the Sabbath
day in every age had been the pledge and foretaste! And yet
the risen Lord told them that they would still have to wait for
the final great Sabbath when the whole earth would share and
rejoice in what was now present before them in the risen Jesus.
They were soon to receive the Holy Spirit with new power and

fulness. Then they were to go forth and proclaim the resurrection, and the presence of the new age, and their witness would be fruitful. But there was a final end still to be waited for, when He himself would "come again" in more manifest power and end for ever all the fruitless travail of this earth. They were to wait for this second coming as the day of the eternal Sabbath, the "rest that remained to the people of God" (Heb. iv.9). They were to go out and spread the Gospel all through the earth, inviting men here and now into the Kingdom, to participate already in the blessing of this eternal Sabbath, and to wait with them for it's final and full manifestation.

In the light of all this, the Apostles were bound to continue keeping the Sabbath, for the Kingdom had still to be waited for from above, but they were bound also to transfer the celebration of their Sabbath, in which they met the risen Christ, to the day of the resurrection of Jesus, the "Lord's day" which is now our Sunday. On this day the risen Jesus seems specially to have come to them during their forty day's experience, as if He wanted it made a special day, and they set it apart as the day on which they would cease from their earthly labours and gather together to realise His presence, share in the joy of His resurrection, give their minds to His Word and celebrate the Lord's Supper.

Yet while they continued to observe a Christian Sabbath on the Lord's day in this way, they never lost sight of the fact that a man most truly fulfilled the Sabbath Commandment, when, in the presence of the risen Jesus Christ, he renounced all trust in his own works, and rejoicing in the forgiveness of sins and the new liberty that Christ had come to give him, surrendered to Him heart and mind and soul and strength, and went forth in the freedom of this experience, to continue his work on earth, in the hope of the final coming of this eternal kingdom.

CHAPTER VI

THE KEEPING OF THE SABBATH

1. The gift of the Sabbath

WE have seen that the Sabbath day is to be understood primarily as the sign of God's gift to us of Himself, of His desire to communicate with us in a new and better way than through creation itself. It is a sign that holds out to men, apart from any work on their part, a participation in His own freedom and joy and rest. Through the Sabbath day, as instituted amongst the Jews in the Old Testament, God sought to draw near to men to give them a communion with Himself that they could not have through the ordinary routine of work and life in this world.

We have seen, too, that the gift of which the Sabbath is a sign is received and responded to adequately only by the complete surrender of the self to God in faith and freedom, as we seek to share in God's sabbath-gift. The true response to God's gift of the Sabbath is to have the faith that renounces all trust in works, and looks to God's grace alone for all man truly needs. The true keeping of the Sabbath is to have the Sabbath in the heart.

2. The keeping of the Sabbath by the Jew

The keeping of the Sabbath in the Old Testament demanded that a total sacrifice of life and work, as well as of heart, should be made to God on the Sabbath day. God did not confine His Sabbath Commandment to a demand for a certain attitude of heart corresponding to His gift. He demanded also from man an outward sign of his inward attitude. This outward sign of inward surrender was the cessation from all work on the Sabbath. This involved a complete interruption of the ordinary routine of his daily life. "The seventh day is the sabbath of the Lord thy God: in it thou shalt not do any work, thou, nor thy servant, nor thy maidservant, nor thy cattle, nor thy stranger that is within thy gates."

The sign of the total surrender of body and spirit here demanded could be given only on the Sabbath day. On all the other days of the week, God's people were called to absorb themselves rightly and sensibly in the toil for existence, the pursuit of culture, and in the processes involved in their necessary co-operation with God's creative activity. Therefore on a weekday there was neither occasion nor opportunity for such a direct sign of surrender to God. But their observance of the Sabbath told God that they indeed sought to respond to His goodness with their whole heart and outward life, that they believed in the coming eternal Sabbath of which the day reminded them, and that they were indeed willing to be detached from their works and from their involvement in the business of the created world in order to receive the best that God was willing to give. "Verily my Sabbaths ye shall keep: for it is a sign between me and you throughout your generations; that ye may know that I am the Lord that doth sanctify you" (Ex. xxxi.13). "Moreover also I gave them my sabbaths, to be a sign between me and them, that they might know that I am the Lord that sanctify them" (Ezek. xx.12).

The Sabbath day, then, brought not only a gift to Israel but a challenge. It called on them to tear themselves apart from the work to which many of them, like ourselves, tended to become devoted, to detach themselves from their weekly and daily programmes and policies, to limit their earthbound schemes and plans, to realise that man did not live by bread alone, and to have faith that God would provide even that bread, when in a season of bad weather the Sabbath might be the only possible day for saving a portion of their scarce crop. To be forced to keep the Sabbath was a sore trial for the unbelieving. The day was a burden to those who trusted in themselves, who wanted to get on with the struggle for life that they thought more important than communion with God. It was a frustrating and futile bar to human progress to those who believed that the true meaning of life was really to be found within the earthly effort of daily toil, and that the Kingdom of God was something to be built on earth. It was a vexing limitation of existence to those who were used to following their own plans and pleasures.

It was, indeed, so difficult truly to keep the Sabbath faithfully in its outward details, that Sabbath observance even in Old Testament times could be interpreted only as arising from the deepest devotion of the heart to God. The Sabbath could be observed as a joyful sacrifice of thanksgiving to God only by those who were detached from themselves and their own pleasures and works (cp. Is. LVIII.13), by those who had made the renunciation of all trust in their own efforts, those who looked for ultimate salvation not from the midst of this world's life but from above and beyond it. But even for such, Sabbath observance demanded hard discipline. It was a day for strict self-denial, for being ready to go not their own way, but God's way. How could anyone yield his life as a sacrifice of thanksgiving, put himself at God's disposal, yield the actual loving obedience demanded by His Word, without very deliberate efforts? Perhaps those who found the Sabbath easiest to keep were the desperate, for whom life on the other days of the week had been emptied of meaning or of fulness.

Yet while God demanded outward Sabbath observance, He made it clear to His people, through the prophets, that it was the true Sabbath attitude of heart that pleased Him more than the forms of outward obedience that marked their keeping of the day. This is why in the Fourth Commandment we have, not a demand for blind literal obedience to an imposed law, but an invitation to understand the meaning and value of a priceless gift and, then, inspired by gratitude, to open the heart and mind and home to its reception. God abominated the superficial observance of those who said, "when will the new moon be gone, that we may sell corn? and the Sabbath that we may set forth wheat?" (Amos VIII.4–6), keeping the day strictly according to the letter, but not in the spirit. He expected His people to "call the Sabbath a delight" (Is. LVIII.13), because they had it in the heart. He expected, too, that the man who had the Sabbath in his heart on the Sabbath day, would continue into all his efforts during the weekday, his attitude of faith, self-denial, and detachment, and that his whole conduct would be marked by a moderation in seeking earthly gain and worldly prosperity.

3. The keeping of the Lord's Day
by the Christian Church

We have seen that early in the Church's life, the Lord's day, rather than the Jewish Sabbath, was made the special day for Christians. The early Christians found the true meaning of the Sabbath fulfilled when they were in the presence of the risen Lord of the Sabbath. They found that the gift and the challenge which the Sabbath was ordained to bring them were presented to them in full reality when the risen Christ came into their midst. Though this Sabbath presence could no longer be thought of as exclusive to any one day, they nevertheless seemed to have a special experience of it weekly, as they were enabled to gather together to celebrate the Lord's resurrection on the day on which it originally occurred (cp. Jn. xx.1, 26; Rev. 1.10; Acts xx.7; 1 Cor. xvi.2).

It is reasonable to believe that the early Christians adopted the same attitude to the Lord's day, as the pious Jews traditionally adopted towards their Sabbath. They sought to keep it as their forefathers in the faith had kept their Sabbath. Though the faith of those who lived in New Testament times was bound, on the whole, to be more powerful and vivid than those who lived in Old Testament times, nevertheless, essentially, the nature of faith, and the nature of the impulse it gives to behaviour are the same, whether in Old Testament times or New Testament, and true faith tends to produce the same expression in practical life whether in the Old or the New Testaments. Therefore when the early Christians read the Old Testament passages appealing for a true attitude towards the Sabbath, and a loyal observance of the day as a day of rest, gladness, and release, they were bound to find them relevant and authoritative as a challenge to Christian behaviour. There are those who think that because the New Testament has few exhortations to Christians about the keeping of the Sabbath, this means that the New Testament Church actually regarded the day as now abolished completely by Christ's fulfilment of it, and the need for keeping any Sabbath as cancelled. But it is more likely that the early Christians found the Sabbath

true faith must find time to get alone with God.

Commandments of the Old Testament so powerful and relevant that they did not need to be further reminded in any other
way to keep their new Sabbath day, or taught how to keep it.
The sabbatising of the Lord's day was the outcome of a witness
they felt it was in their hearts to give to the significance of
Jesus Christ, and its observance was the expression of an in-
ward-felt necessity on their part. The accounts we have, seem
to suggest that on the Lord's day, as far as the exigencies of
their station in life allowed, they instinctively abstained from
their normal pursuits and celebrated their worship, especially
the Lord's Supper, with great joy and intense expectancy of
the second coming of Christ, giving themselves to meditation,
preaching, instruction in the faith, and also to the distribution
of alms and food to those who had need. Certainly the inward
aspect and meaning of the outward keeping the Sabbath was
bound to be stressed in the early Church even more than in the
Old Testament.

In connexion with their teaching on the observance of the
Lord's day, the early Church must have learned from the story
of Martha and Mary which is preserved for us in the Gospel
of Luke (Lk. x.38–42). When Jesus visited that home,
obviously with something on His mind that He wanted them
to hear, and something in His heart that He wanted to share
with them, Mary alone dropped the routine of her work and
sat at his feet. She relaxed completely and very deliberately,
for she must have known well that she was facing unpleasant
criticism and inevitable misunderstanding from Martha. But
to her, the visit of Jesus was like the breaking in of a true Sabbath into their home. While He was there she must deliberately
observe the Sabbath. She became receptive and worshipful and
put herself completely at His disposal as far as she could read
His mind. If He had asked her to work, and had expressed His
desire for a meal she would have worked as hard as Martha at
preparing it. How foolish Martha showed herself in contrast to
Mary! In face of this Sabbath opportunity she could not relax,
and become free from her work in order to share in what Jesus
has to give her through it. Did she not believe more in her work
than in the grace that Jesus brought to her? The result was that
she had no understanding of what He really wanted from her

there and then. She misinterpreted Him completely. She had
no Sabbath in her heart, therefore she could not respond to
Him with a real Sabbath release, gladness, and rest. Jesus
reproached Martha for exaggerating the importance of her
bustling activity. Even though she might be doing it in an
attempt to please Him, she had completely misunderstood what
He wanted and required from her at that moment. Mary was
praised by Jesus as having chosen "that better part," and we
are to learn from her rather than from Martha, how Jesus
wants us, whatever the age we live in, to respond to His
visitation of us in our worship and in our homes on the Lord's
day. Perhaps even His promise that what Mary had chosen
in contrast to Martha, "shall not be taken away from her" was
used against those in the early Church who suggested that since
Jesus had fulfilled the Sabbath promise in His coming, there
was no need any more in the Church for Sabbath observance
of any kind.

It comes out clearly in the story of Martha and Mary that
an essential feature in all true Sabbath observance must be
Mary's Sabbath attitude. Out own outward keeping of the
Sabbath must be inspired by our letting the Sabbath first possess the heart as Mary did, and this in contrast to Martha. It
is only through the adoring receptivity of faith and its detachment from trust in works, that we can be enabled on the
Sabbath day to drop our work from the heart in real detachment and release from the tension of the world's round of
business and to turn ourselves wholeheartedly to God.

For us, no less than for the Jew, what matters for the keeping
of the Sabbath is primarily the total surrender of the heart to
God. But the surrender of the heart, if it is genuine, will carry
with it the surrender of the outward life. "I beseech you therefore, brethren, by the mercies of God, that ye present your
bodies a living sacrifice, holy, acceptable unto God, which is
your reasonable service" (Rom. xii.1). We must ask ourselves
if the Gospel in this respect can face us on the Lord's day with
a challenge any less totalitarian than that made on the Jew
in the Old Testament by the coming of the Sabbath? If our
trust is placed not in our own works but in God's grace alone
and we seek the Kingdom not through our own efforts but

through His promise, this will tend to express itself on the Sabbath day in the dropping of all work, in the relaxation from the tension of every aspect of the weekday, and in a gladness to sacrifice the profits and gains and prizes that our giving of the Sunday to God involves. Surely, too, we will tend to forego our own programmes of pleasure and sport which are often so self-appointed, and, after all really belong to the round of Monday to Saturday, being simply part of the necessary weekday complement of our weekday labour. But such renunciation and relaxation will be made primarily in order to make room for worship, fellowship, loving service, instruction in, and discussion of, the faith, and evangelism.

In the response we make on the Sabbath, we are bound to remember that for us too, no less than for the Jew, a mere form of outward obedience, without the devotion of the heart, is an abomination to God. It becomes a sheer act of hypocrisy to attend church, to keep strictly to an outward routine in obedience to what we imagine is a rigid law, if at the same time even in the midst of our Church services we can take out our watches and look at them, as if our own time, and our own appointments of which we have six days full every week already, must still somehow dominate this day too.

Surely it is a far more serious matter to grudge the minister a little over twenty minutes to proclaim the everlasting Gospel on the day when we are commanded not to live under bondage to the processes of time, than to play football in the public parks! The real serious Sabbath-breaking under the New Testament is done as much in the heart as in the outward behaviour.

Moreover, if our keeping of the Sabbath is indeed a sign of the faith we have in our hearts, and this faith accompanies us from Monday to Saturday into our week's work, pleasure and relaxation, it is bound to express itself in a certain detachment from the world's scramble after profits and position, in a certain lack of concern over earthly prizes and rewards. The "good part" which Mary chose could not be "taken away" from her (Lk. x.42), and the same faith that makes the Christian give the outward sign of complete surrender of the whole life to God on the Sabbath day, will also enable him spontaneously and naturally to give corresponding signs during the ordinary course of life, that reveal at times whether or not the Sabbath is there in the heart.

4. The universalising and legalising of the Sabbath by Church and State

The Lord's day, as an institution, tends to universalise itself. As the Church kept the Christian Sabbath, it was found that the mere keeping of it as a day of relaxation and rest, was by itself, and quite apart from any serious understanding of its meaning, a good thing both for the Church, as an institution, and for the individual. Especially where the weekdays were given to really hard and sometimes very pointless and unprofitable labour, it was psychologically a good thing to have one day in which the burden was lifted, the vision enlarged, another and better purpose grasped, and the limitations of life seen in their true proportions. It was organisationally a good thing for the Church to have one day on which all its members could come together for common fellowship and instruction, for prayer and the enterprises of evangelism and service.

Moreover it became clear that the Sabbath was a good thing not only for the Church on Christian grounds, but also for all men even on natural grounds. The refusal to work one day each week, was obviously a healthy safeguard for the worker. It helped to prevent physical and nervous breakdowns, and certain forms of exploitation of labour. It was good for family life. It served to remind men that life was not given merely to be sacrificed to earthly toil. The Christians themselves were bound to remember that Jesus was Lord of all men, and when He said, "The Sabbath was made for man," He did not qualify the word "man"; God meant all men to share, if even partially, in the blessing given to men through the institution of the Sabbath, and to come to understand themselves and life better, because of it. Therefore where it has been observed by the Church, the Sunday has always tended to become part of the life of the people or society in the midst of which the Church has lived and witnessed. The world has tended to copy the

Church. Shops have begun to close, trading to cease, employment to be relaxed, on this one day each week.

Along with this universalising process there has also been a legalising process. The Sabbath attitude of mind tended to express itself in certain patterns of Sabbath behaviour amongst Christians, and gradually those ways of behaviour become traditional. An accepted code of Sabbath behaviour arose, on the basis of the Fourth Commandment, this code came to be regarded as a law prescribing particular behaviour, and came to be interpreted legalistically rather than evangelically. Moreover, within the State, the Sabbath began to be established and protected by laws as part of the life of the whole community.

5. The preservation of the Sabbath

On many sides today a demand is heard for the repeal of some of the legislation in the statute book that protects the traditional Sunday, for more Sunday freedom for sport and entertainment than has been customary, and for a more liberal attitude within the Church with respect to Sabbath observance. Those who find Sunday restrictions irksome ask if Christians have any right to impose their views of the Sabbath, or indeed their Sabbath in any form, on the rest of the community. Within the Church there has been a good deal of bewilderment as to whether the movement demanded is good or bad, and as to how far the Church dare co-operate or resist.

It must be frankly recognised that the motives behind such a movement are not always healthy. The exaggerated descriptions of the Sabbath tradition in Scotland, for instance, which are used sometimes to support such change, are given often by those who resent other healthy features of their Christian heritage. Many of the proposed "encroachments" on the traditional Sabbath are inspired by the desire of commercial interests to cash in on what, if restrictions could be more easily relaxed, would obviously be a hitherto unworked gold-mine. In face of all this, we have a right to point to a great deal that is obviously good and healthy from the point of view of the community, in our Sunday tradition. For this purpose we can search and find that nearly all the great statesmen of every political party in the past, have at some time or other spoken eloquently of the benefit our traditional Sunday has brought to the life of Britain.

The attempt to "preserve the Lord's day" however, merely by political agitation and by appeal to law and tradition, will ultimately be in vain. Our main concern and policy in seeking to preserve the Lord's day must be the revival of a living witness on this matter by the members of the Church, and by a more vigorous effort to evangelise and serve those who are now not simply outside the Christian faith, but growing more and more alien to the Christian tradition. The best way for Christians to preserve the Sunday is for Christians "to remember the Sabbath day to keep it holy." What the world needs in order to convince it that a Sabbath day is worth having is to see in its midst a community of men and women who really find a living meaning in the keeping of this day.

It is because the Church itself has lost its vision of the meaning of the Sabbath day for its own faith, that it is unable to convince the outsider that the Sabbath can possibly have any significance for himself. The Sabbath day must be looked at afresh by us and seen in a new light. We must cease to regard it as the point at which God challenges us about obedience to His laws, or as the point at which we come up against an unyielding element in the constitution of the universe against which we will be broken up if we ignore it. We must, rather, recapture a vision of it as the day on which God, in His pure grace seeks to give us a fresh chance to become delivered from our self-seeking by His love, and enables us to express and exercise certain aspects of our faith in a way for which we have no normal opportunities when we are caught up in the routine of Monday to Saturday. We must return to Christ to receive His "rest", and then for us the "day of rest" will become the day on which we find ourselves most free to express to the world in a new way by praise and service the glorious liberty and destiny of the children of God.

THE FIFTH COMMANDMENT

EXODUS xx. 12. *Honour thy father and thy mother, that thy days may be long upon the land which the Lord thy God giveth thee.*

Chapter VII

THE FREEDOM TO BUILD

1. The Promise

(i) God's long-term policy in the midst of history

MUCH of the Old Testament is taken up with the story of a promise, and its fulfilment. When God called Abraham out of Ur of the Chaldees to go to a "land that I will shew thee," He promised, "I will make of thee a great nation, and I will bless thee, and make thy name great; and thou shalt be a blessing . . . and in thee shall all the families of the earth be blessed" (Gen. xii.1–3). The same promise was repeated in different forms to Jacob and his successors, and then to Moses when he was sent to lead the people out of Egypt. All the time of their wanderings in the wilderness, the promise of the land of their future, and the blessings, both for themselves and for all men, which God would give them in it, sustained their hope and courage. "We are journeying unto the place of which the Lord said, I will give it you" (Num. x.29), was Moses' summary at that time of the hope that sustained himself and his people throughout all their disappointments, trials, and battles. In this land to which they were going, they believed that God had some great purpose to work out for the whole world through their faithfulness and obedience. In it God was going to give them rest (Deut. xxv.19). Here at the heart of the Ten Commandments they are reminded of it again—and as they are reminded of it, they are also reminded that it will come to its fulfilment only when century has followed century, and their days have been "long" upon the land.

Today we have no difficulty in understanding what God meant when He gave Israel the promise "thy days shall be long in the land." The great event that was to take place in the land of the promise, was the birth, life, death, and resurrection of Jesus, and the unfolding in Him of the meaning of man's

creation and of God's eternal purpose for all things. This was
the purpose God was working out through the long discipline
of His people in the land which He gave them to possess. This
was the blessing through which He was going to bless not only
them but all mankind. It was to happen only after centuries of
struggle, disappointment, toil, delay, frustration, testing, education, prayer, and hidden preparation of attitude. But, at last,
at the right time, and in the very place chosen and promised,
God fulfilled His purpose, and Jesus was born. As we read
through the Old Testament, we find its history, and its stories,
full of new purpose and meaning when we see it all moving
towards the fulfilment of this promise in Jesus, and we can see
how in many of the details of the story God was majestically
and slowly at work, making everything contribute to this great
and crowning fulfilment, even from the earliest times, and even
when His people were in a rebellious mood, unwilling to
co-operate or believe.

(ii) *The aspects of the promise that are still in force*

God is still continuing to work out the purpose He began
when he gave the promise to Israel. Even the great events of
the birth, life, death, and resurrection of Jesus did not complete
what God purposed when He delivered Israel from Egypt.
Since the death, resurrection, and ascension of Jesus, God has
started a new phase of His operations in this world. He is now
working towards another great event at another appointed
time. This time is called in Scripture by various names, but
most often it is referred to as the "day of the Lord"—a day
towards which everything that occurs in human history is
straining, and is being directed in a hidden way to make its
contribution. The sphere within which God is personally
conducting this new phase of His operation within history is
now greatly enlarged, compared with that in the Old Testament. No longer is His main attention concentrated on one
little area of the earth. His purpose is being actively worked out
in the whole world, and the force He has commissioned and
sent out, as He prepares the whole world for this event, is now
not simply one nation, but a universal Church, a people

gathered out of every nation, and made one body by the out-pouring of His spirit upon it at Pentecost.

This makes the promise of the Fifth Commandment directly relevant to us in the Church today. As God gave Israel the sure promise that they would possess their land, so He has given the Church both the promise that it will possess the world, and the command to do so. As the Church seeks to fulfil this pur-pose, its protection and prosperity, its further discipline and correction, are still the supreme concern of God. When Christ sent out His disciples on their mission to go everywhere on earth and make disciples of all nations, He promised them the same fellowship, protection, and success as God promised to Israel in the Fifth Commandment. "Go ye therefore and teach all nations . . . and, lo, I am with you alway, even unto the end of the world" (Mt. xxviii.19–20). "Fear not little flock for it is your Father's good pleasure to give you the Kingdom" (Lk. xii.32). In the Gospels we have a vivid picture of His constant care for His disciples' welfare in body as well as in spirit, of the way He never failed to come into their midst in their time of distress or danger or failure, to see them through each crisis as it occurred. In all this we have a picture of the never failing care which, throughout all ages, He will give to the Church as it goes forth into the midst of this world's life and history, seeking in its weakness to fulfil His command to possess the world for Him, and to be the instruments through which He can fulfil His purpose amongst all nations.

2. Inheriting the promise

(i) *The faith that Israel invested in the historical task*

The promise of this commandment brought a great challenge to the faith of the people of Israel. Those who received it from Moses in the wilderness must have wondered if they could ever possibly enter the land of the promise at all. The obstacles before them were insurmountable. As a nation they were few in number, and untrained in the methods of warfare by which nomadic people normally survive in the desert struggle for existence. Surely the future of the world lay more in what God was doing in the midst of the life of the great surrounding empires, than in what He could possibly do with them in the land to which they were going! They were to find the land, when they came to it, already populated by tribes and races who had a native right to it, and who were so deeply entrenched in their fortresses that it seemed impossible that they could ever be removed. Yet time and again the Word of God spoke to them, constantly challenging them to believe that this very land was being reserved for them by God. Their days were to be "long" upon it. It was the place God had chosen as the scene of the fulfilment of His covenant with the whole of creation. And ultimately, when the time God had chosen arrived, the event which would prove to be the climax of all their national life and the blessing of all nations would take place.

At times, the response of many of them to this apparently impossible command to go and possess this land, was magnificent—even though they often made mistakes in their interpretation of the details of the part they themselves were to play in fulfilling it. When they came out of Egypt they knew no more about the real nature of the purpose to which the career of their nation was to be dedicated than did Abraham, when he was called out of Ur of the Chaldees and went forth "not knowing whither he went." But in the midst of their dim and wild guesses at what this future might hold for them and all mankind, they found themselves nevertheless challenged constantly to reject all the cynicism, despair, and weariness that might discourage them from the pursuit of its fulfilment. As God called them to go forward they obeyed, believing that He would open up the way, and give them the victory over every difficulty. When they arrived in Canaan they dwelt there, settled down, built up and nourished their national and religious life around this faith in their future. When they were driven out into exile, they never lost faith that there they would return once more. When they came back to find devastation and ruin around them, they rebuilt with new faith that on this earth, and in this particular land, God's glory would yet be revealed, and that in spite of all man's failure and sin, not one of the promises would fail, and God's people would never be ashamed.

Their whole career as a nation was a struggle never to let go

of this faith, to keep hold of the promises by which it was
nourished, and to submit to the hand of God, whether it
chastised them or blessed them, believing that all things would
work together in His providence to fulfil His word to them. In
face of all the difficulties, and throughout centuries of waiting,
they made their mark in the land, and staked their claim for
God in the midst of this world's history. They lived in obedience
to the very earthly vision conjured up by this promise, toiling,
suffering, struggling, always believing that, because of their own
history, all human history too would find its meaning and its
goal through the faith given to them by God.

(ii) Our mood of unsettlement

A current philosophy of our day encourages us to live only
for the present moment. Neither the past nor the future, we are
told, are real. In any case there is the bomb. Is it worth while
even thinking of living and planning for any distant tomorrow,
when we know there are enough madmen in the world to
ensure that our nuclear stock piles will be used? Does not all
that we can learn from contemporary history reinforce such
questioning? Much of what was "solid building for the future"
collapsed during the War, in the mass destruction of buildings,
political institutions, and other monuments of man's patient
devotion and Christian culture. The same process of disin-
tegration and change is still eating away at much that seemed
good in the established life of the Churches in Europe. The
potentialities today in the hand of evil for destroying all traces
of any Christian heritage are more powerful than ever they
were. It is only too easy for anti-Christian forces, served by
modern scientific methods of overcoming psychological resistance, and by modern means of mass communication, to fulfil
deliberate policies aimed at undermining everything that the
Church might try to build within history.

We are tempted simply to lift up our eyes towards heaven
to comfort ourselves that the Kingdom of God is safe up there,
and to forget about its relation to the course of history on earth.
Therefore we indulge freely in Apocalyptic thinking. Perhaps,
indeed, the end of the world will come in our time! In this case,
we imagine, planning for the long term future of the Church

does not matter so much as it once did. We have lost our zeal
to struggle, as our fathers did, against the evil tendencies of
mind, attitude, and behaviour that are always rooting themselves and growing with vigour in the world around us. We
feel that the battle for "Christendom" or the battle to vindicate
any form of Christian outlook against modern paganism is not
so urgent as it once was. The conviction grows that all that
matters is to save souls, and to introduce the individual in the
midst of his pagan environment to a pious experience of Jesus.
Existential encounter is better than education. The desire for
quick results, and for flashy momentary "experiences," expresses itself often in a contempt for the long term, and often
painful, theological discussions that are necessary if the Church
is to give new form to its teachings in order that the Gospel
should make its full impact on the growing mind. The contempt for "the establishment" manifest in political and social
discussion is reflected in a contempt for the establishment
and continuance of forms of Church life and discipline.

Our situation today becomes analogous to that prevailing
in the Church at Thessalonica where the Christians were so
excitedly taken up with the prospect of the second coming, in
addition to being overcome by the difficulties that obviously
faced them in the task of Church-building, that they became
careless even in attending to their own daily work. Words
written by Dietrich Bonhoeffer in Germany under Hitler,
describing a western state of mind, are still relevant. "Everything established is threatened with annihilation. This is not a
crisis among other crises. It is a decisive struggle of the last days.
The Western world senses the uniqueness of the moment at
which it stands, and it throws itself into the arms of the void,
while the Christians talk among themselves of the approach of
the day of judgment. . . . In face of the peril of the void, there
is no longer any meaning in the question of the historical
inheritance which requires of those who receive it that they
shall both develop it in the present and hand it on to the future.
There is no future and there is no past. There is only the
moment which has been rescued from the void, and the desire
to snatch from the void the next moment as well. Already what
belongs to yesterday is consigned to oblivion and the affairs of

tomorrow are too far off to impose any obligation today. . . .
Nothing makes a permanent impression and nothing imposes
a lasting obligation" (*Ethics* pp. 41–2).

(iii) The challenge to "build and to plant"

The promise of this Commandment must be allowed to
jerk us out of this retreating and despairing mood. Even in face
of the bomb, and the disappointments of the past, even in face
of the fact that the Church finds itself again to be a minority
body, a small nation, in the midst of huge alien world forces,
we have a historical task to fulfil in the light of the promise that
our days will be long upon the earth which the Lord has given
us to possess. It is not only the present moment that is under
the control and concern of God, but also the course of history
and the destiny of men and nations on this earth. It is revealed
in Christ's resurrection that there is a stable foundation in the
ordering of this universe on which building for the future is
"not in vain." There is an historical purpose which God, even
in the midst of apparent historical chaos, is working out, though
its unfolding is often hidden in mystery.

Our task like that of the prophets of Israel is "to build and
to plant" (Jer. 1.10) as well as to proclaim a crisis, and call for
decision. It is to reap and to sow within the processes of earth's
history, and thus make a mark there as well as in the eternal
Kingdom of God.

It is true that we have to learn to live for the present moment
as well as for the future. In showing us the meaning of life,
Jesus Christ has filled our present with meaning, as well as our
future. Through Him God has made the present sweet and
challenging, and has filled it with an urgency and significance
it could not have apart from Him. The Book of Ecclesiastes and
The Song of Solomon surely bear witness to this fact. It is true,
also, that we have to learn to live for something greater than
can be contained either in the present moment or in the future
of this earth. This life, within the uncertainties of history, is not
big enough to give full scope to the faith and hope that the
Word of God gives to the human heart.

But whatever else we live, look for, and find satisfaction in,
we must also live and toil for the earthly future of our Church

and world in our own lifetime, and in the generations that may
lie ahead. We must do this in faith in the continuance of human
history. In face of preparations for nuclear war, we must refuse
to despair of the future of the race. In face of the gloomy analyses
of the processes which seem to spell doom to our Western
civilisation, we must still believe that with God all things are
possible, even for the continuance of the world and the Church
we know and love.

When the Jewish exiles in Babylon were being tempted to
lose faith in the significance of their earthly future, and were
giving way to restless despair, Jeremiah wrote them commanding them to settle down even in Babylon, in faith that God
meant them to make the best they could of a difficult earthly
situation, through living still for the promise that would lead
them through it.

"Thus saith the Lord of hosts, the God of Israel, unto all
that are carried away captives, whom I have caused to be
carried away from Jerusalem unto Babylon; Build ye houses,
and dwell in them; and plant gardens, and eat the fruit of them;
Take ye wives, and beget sons and daughters; and take wives
for your sons, and give your daughters to husbands, that they
may bear sons and daughters; that ye may be increased there,
and not diminished. And seek the peace of the city whither I
have caused you to be carried away captives, and pray unto
the Lord for it: for in the peace thereof shall ye have peace"
(Jer. xxix.4-7).

One can understand how much significance the Christians
behind the Iron Curtain, especially in East Germany, have
found in these words today. One can see how important it is,
in face of a constantly challenging Communist regime, for the
Church to learn to settle down and build for the future, and to
work out the new form both of its own salvation, and of its
service to a partly alien government. It is equally important
for us, on the other side of the Iron Curtain, also to learn to
refuse to resign our responsibility for the earthly future.

(iv) The sober realism of faith

There is a sober realism in the New Testament about the
daemonic possibilities that threaten to embody themselves in

earthly rule, and to produce, within this world, government forces of Anti-Christ destructive of the good, the beautiful, and the human, and antagonistic to the Church. There is, also however, in face of these possibilities, no matter how far they have developed, a sober realism about our need for building up our Church life, for the Christian nurture and training of the young, and for a long-term Christian missionary policy. There is no reason to suppose, as too many New Testament critics do, in their desire to have everything neat and logical, that this latter note was not sounded originally in the teaching of Jesus itself, and that with all His apocalyptic emphasis (*e.g.*, Mk. xiii), He did not envisage also the continuing life of a Church on earth. "All things are yours," said Paul, "whether . . . the world, or life, or death, or things present, or things to come" (i Cor. iii.22). When he included "the world" and "life" in this list of "all things" belonging to the Christian, he was surely re-echoing for the Christians of his day, the Old Testament command to possess their earthly inheritance.

For the Church, the command "to build and to plant" in the midst of human history, and to "possess the land" which God gives to it, must mean the constant effort by the congregation in any given area to seek to win the whole "parish" within which it is placed. It must mean the setting up of the closest possible relationship between Church and people. And this can lead to a very close relationship between Church and State. It means a stress on patient Christian education as well as fervent evangelism. It means, for the individual Christian, a consciousness of being called to wield in every possible way a humble yet loving influence in trades unions, professional organisations, and in every sphere in which God places him. It must mean a concern for co-operation with all Christians in the struggle against the enemies of the Gospel, and a will to work for ultimate Church unity. How can we ignore the call to seek one Church on earth, if we have any vision of a historical future in which God is working out His purpose through the Church?

But for the accomplishment of all this, Christians require constantly to strengthen their faith in the real and lasting nature of the inheritance which will be given to the Church in this earth as long as human history continues. Only such faith will enable the Church constantly to rise up again, hopeful and strong after those periods when evil and chaotic forces seem to be allowed to destroy much of its Christian inheritance. To quote Bonhoeffer again: "Even while she waits for the last day, the Church, as the bearer of a historical inheritance, is bound by an obligation to the historical future. Her vision of the end of all things must not hinder her in the fulfilment of her historical responsibility. She must leave not only the end to God's decision, but also the possibility of the continuance of history" (*Ethics*, p. 45).

The stronger the Church's faith in its historical inheritance, the more will it tend to guard within itself the practice of infant Baptism. Certainly there must be other grounds than this particular one for continuing this practice, and its validity must often be re-examined. But if God has an historical role for His Church to fulfil within the continuation of human history, then the children of the families which make up the Church are obviously involved in a greater responsibility for the fulfilment of this purpose than those of other families and the obvious sign of their election to this responsibility and privilege, is their being baptised into membership of the people of God, and into the close relationship to Christ through which this purpose can alone be fulfilled. We can baptise our children in the confident faith that God has not annulled His Old Testament promises to continue through the children the work He has begun to do through the fathers, and has not cancelled His gracious attitude to the children of those who serve Him and believe in Him.

CHAPTER VIII

THE FREEDOM TO INHERIT

1. The service of the promise by tradition and family

THE Fifth Commandment makes it clear that the long-term purpose of God in the midst of human history can be powerfully served by tradition, and that family life, in particular, is the sphere in which God seeks the service of this tradition.

"One generation shall praise thy name to another, and shall declare thy mighty acts" (Ps. CXLV.4). Unless this takes place, all other service that outstanding individuals might give to God's promise and purpose is in vain. It would have been vain had Abraham spent his life in sacrifice, prayer, and toil and yet had neglected to tell Isaac and his children and his household of the wonder and meaning of the promise and of how it could best be served within their family loyalty. "Abraham shall surely become a great and mighty nation, and all the nations of the earth shall be blessed in him. For I know him, that he will command his children and his household after him and they shall keep the way of the Lord, and do justice and judgment; that the Lord may bring upon Abraham that which he hath spoken of him" (Gen. XVIII,18–19). Those in Israel who know God's purpose, and understand it even faintly, will find it burning in their hearts to speak of it to each other, and especially to the generation rising up around them. Those who understand the meaning of the law with its promises will give heed to God's special admonition, without obedience to which all the other Commandments will be in vain: "And these words which I command thee this day, shall be in thine heart: and thou shalt teach them diligently unto thy children, and shalt talk of them when thou sittest in thine house, and when thou walkest by the way, and when thou liest down, and when thou risest up. And thou shalt bind them for a sign upon thine hand, and they shall be as frontlets between thine eyes. And thou shalt write them upon the posts of thy house, and on thy gates" (Deut. vi.6–9).

In a multitude of different ways, God makes one generation of His people depend upon another. For instance, God spoke His Word to the men of each generation of the children of Israel, revealed Himself to them in His unreserved love, and sought to communicate to them as much light as they could bear in the frailty of their understanding. But the earlier generations did not understand or grasp so fully as the later ones, what God was giving them in His revelation of Himself. The later generations were helped to come to a better understanding of what they were given by God, and a firmer and fuller grasp of it, by the experiences and insights and even by the mistakes of the previous generations as they had wrestled with the Word of God. The understanding which one generation has of the truth that comes to it, even directly from God, is "always conditioned by the hearing and understanding of previous generations" (T. F. Torrance, *The School of Faith*, pp. lxvii). There is undoubtedly within the Bible itself, if not a progressive revelation, at least a growing understanding of the meaning of what God is saying through His Word to Israel. This understanding continuously increases in breadth and depth, as each generation does its thinking, proves God in its experience, learns from its mistakes. What each has learned is to be passed on to those who come after, in a gradually growing crystallisation of wisdom and prudence as each generation of the community lives under the Word of God.

But all this itself could not take place unless there is an Isaac to follow Abraham. The latter's concern to have a son was not simply for His own satisfaction and pleasure, but for the sake of the promise. It is this fact that explains why, in the Old Testament, childlessness was regarded as such a heavy burden and large families as such a blessing. We must notice that this attitude has no prominence in the New Testament. Today it is more possible for those who have no children, according to the flesh, to have spiritual children, and to be indeed true fathers and mothers within the life of the Church (1 Tim. 1.2; Gal. iv.19).

Though the tension on this matter for the individual is

today so obviously relaxed, there is justification for pointing out to Christian married couples, however, that a deliberate refusal to raise up children who can grow in grace and in the knowledge of God, can be a tragic failure to fulfil the purpose which a Christian's home life is meant to serve. One can understand that, with some who are tempted to make this refusal, the motive may be that of sheer horror at the thought of plunging a new and innocent human life into a world that is seriously threatened with nuclear terror and death. But is this a possible Christian attitude in the light of the resurrection of Jesus Christ from the dead? Psalm cxxvii has still some relevance for Christians (though we will not think of laying the same stress on the size of the quiver as is made in the Old Testament). "Lo, children are an heritage of the Lord: and the fruit of the womb is his reward. As arrows are in the hand of a mighty man; so are children of the youth. Happy is the man that hath his quiver full of them" (Ps. cxxvii. 3-5).

2. The handing on of the promise by the passing generation

It is obviously not enough merely to have a "quiver-full"! The Psalm which brought this desirability before the people of its day also stressed the fact that the arrows, so bountifully provided by God, had to be shot into the future, and that their trajectory had to be deliberately chosen for them by those into whose "mighty" hands they had been providentially placed. "As arrows in the hand of a mighty man; so are the children of youth" (Ps. cxxvii). It is the hands of the parents which are "mighty" in this respect. So highly does the Bible estimate the power of parents in this respect that with obvious exceptions (even the prodigal son had a good father) the sins of the younger generation are laid at the door of the older generation, and likewise, again with exceptions (Jonathan in many ways vastly contrasts with Saul), the parents are given the credit for the well-doing of the children. Even in the case of the prodigal in the far country, it was because he remembered the father that he came back (Lk. xv.17).

The unconscious influence of the parents or the "atmosphere"

of the home plays a large part in the working out of God's purpose in this matter. If the parents have God's words on their
own hearts, and make them "frontlets" to their own eyes, and
make them naturally and sensibly a main theme of reference in
the life of the home, then the children will overhear (Deut.
vi.6–9), and the things which are overheard are powerful
factors in a growing life. But it is a wild exaggeration to say
that "religion is not taught, but caught." Stress is also laid in
the Bible on diligent instruction, the commanding, the conscious "nurture and admonition" of the young (Gen. xviii.
18–19; Ex. xii. 26–7; Eph. vi.4). But here it is recognised that
the formal instruction is less powerful than the "admonition"
arising out of particular situations of danger, crisis, and temptation in which the parent finds himself vitally bound up with
the child, and has to utter spontaneous warnings or make
deeply-felt assessments.

But the rising generation must not only be given information,
instruction, and admonition by the passing generation. They
must be brought to faith, and indeed to Christ Himself. The
parents who in the Gospels brought their young children to
Jesus understood this better than we ourselves sometimes do.
They brought them "that He should touch them," and understanding exactly what they wanted, "He took them up in His
arms, put his hands upon them, and blessed them" (Mk.
x.13, 16). It is surely no less than this, along with the tremendous spiritual reality that lies behind the outward sign,
that a Christian parent will seek for a child. They must be
introduced in a very individual and personal way into the
blessing of Christ's fellowship. They must receive from Him
within the divine communion of His Church, the cleansing
and renewal that He bestows upon the faith that comes to Him,
and seeks to touch Him.

What forced and enabled the parents in the Gospels to bring
their young children to Jesus, was obviously a spirit of real
concern and prayer. This concern and prayer were so strong
that they easily withstood even the rebuffs of the Apostles.
Such concern and prayer are there, of course, in an early form
when the children are infants, but they arise again in a much
stronger form when all instruction and admonition have failed

to do anything. No reader of the Gospels can escape the fact that some of Jesus' miracles of cleansing and renewal were accomplished on children brought to Him simply through the anxiety or desperation of parents. Even though they would not or could not come to Him themselves, they were carried to Him, or He was pressed to go to them. All these stories are still completely relevant to the problems and tensions that arise where there is a growing family in the ordinary home today. They were meant to have this relevance in every age (cp. Mk. v.21–43, IX.14–29; Mt. xv.21–8). When Monica in her desperation over her son Augustine, went to consult Bishop Ambrose, he was justified in replying to her "It is impossible that the son of these tears should perish."

We cannot fail to notice that in the matter of being brought to Jesus and blessed by Him, most often the children are in the hands of the parents. It is true that sometimes friends are around also. Sometimes outsiders come in here and take a more prominent part than the parents themselves. Elisha was so influenced by Elijah that he called him "my Father" (II Kings II.12). Eli became almost a father to Samuel in the temple (I Sam. III). But, generally speaking, of what significance is the influence of Eli, compared with that of Hannah, in determining the destiny of Samuel? The Sunday school may still have a valuable place to play in our Church life today, yet it is a pity that it consists often in youngsters teaching other youngsters, and thus does not lead to a real intercourse between the generations. Moreover, it is regrettable that formal "religious instruction" in school and Sunday school has tended to become divorced from a personal concern in actually bringing the instructed into a living relationship of faith to the Christ about whom instruction is being given, and that more stress is sometimes laid on instruction methods than on the pastoral care of the instructed.

3. The receiving of the promise by the rising generation

It would be tragedy and loss indeed, if any generation faced with the gift of such an inheritance of experience and promise,

should like Esau (Gen. xxv.34) despise its birthright, should act
as though it did not need to learn, and should try to work out,
on its own, every problem confronting it. Therefore, within
Israel God seeks to turn the hearts of the children to the fathers.
It is here that the Fifth Commandment finds its most direct
application. "Honour thy father and thy mother that thy days
may be long upon the land which the Lord thy God giveth
thee."

The Commandment emphasises the stability that the generations of Israel will find in observing this appeal to bind themselves in mind, heart, and soul to their fathers. Lasting purpose,
strength, and rest are to be found only in giving heed to the
tradition that is centred on God's promise. Jeremiah under-
lined this point in his message to his own day. "Stand ye in the
ways, and see," he cried to a generation who were being
tempted radically to break with the past amongst the attrac-
tions of untried forms of worship and living, "and ask for the
old paths where is the good way, and walk therein, and ye shall
find rest for your souls" (Jer. vi.16). When we forsake the tradition that God's promises have created within the life of our
community we forsake stability. The psalmist, too, was forced
to admit this, when he confessed, in the seventy-third psalm,
that by allowing himself to stray too far into a morass of
doubts, he had unnecessarily cut himself off from the unfailing
stability of the generations of the people of God, and thus had
sinned. "If I say, I will speak thus; behold I should offend
against the generation of thy children" (Ps. LXXIII.15).

To obey this Commandment, according to Jeremiah, does
not simply mean the blind unquestioning obedience of child
to parent under every circumstance. We are to "ask of the old
paths what is that good way." Father's and Mother's ways can
be bad ways, and the rising generation is given the right to
make a judgment. But they *must* ask. As the problems of life
grow more complicated, as the new situations arise, a constant inquiry must take place from the rising to the passing
generation. This must be especially an inquiry about God, His
Word, and its ways and meaning. This is brought out well in
the story of Samuel in the temple. Eli was in many ways unworthy to be a guide to the rising generation. He must have

seemed senile and stupid and compromised in the eyes of any idealistic youth. Yet God made Samuel depend, for his understanding of the Word He was speaking to him, on the guidance of this Eli, even though the very advice that was required from Eli had to be eventually dragged out of him (cp. 1 Sam. 1.3). Such inquiry as Samuel made to Eli, and the genuine willingness to learn on which it is based, must characterise each rising generation of God's people. The promise and its fulfilment are bound up with such willingness. "And it shall come to pass, when ye come to the land which the Lord will give you, according as he hath promised, that ye shall keep this service. And it shall come to pass, when your children shall say unto you, What mean ye by this service? That ye shall say, It is the sacrifice of the Lord's passover, who passed over the houses of the children of Israel in Egypt" (Ex. XII.26–7).

It is little wonder then, that the commandment runs: "honour thy father and thy mother," without any qualification as to whether father or mother are in themselves good or bad, worthy or unworthy, blameless or criminal—and how can any of us replace our parents by any other? It is by God's grace within Israel, that even a poor father has at least something to pass on to his children. Here is an aspect of life that could almost be called sacramental, and it would be tragic and foolish to refuse to receive one of God's gracious sacraments because the minister is an unworthy man. Here human sin cannot obscure or hinder the grace of God.

Certainly there are great difficulties presented in cases where the parental tie causes humiliation to a child instead of honour, and where the interpretation of the Commandment gives rise to a tyrannous demand that would exclude any free response. We must decide such cases in the light of the fact that it is largely adult obedience within real freedom that is stressed here, an obedience that is accompanied at the same time with inquiry and responsible thinking. Moreover the main reference in this Commandment is to the binding of one generation of Israel to another in the furtherance of God's promise to the whole people. We must allow that this command can be honoured, and yet room also left for real tension between children and parents, as long as such tension is held on the basis of a continuing tradition in which the inheritance of the promise is really being passed on and received.

Freedom must also be reserved for the necessity of ignoring or departing from the traditions of a former generation where these are found to have distorted the real meaning of the promise. In this case to "honour" is to disobey, and Jesus Himself though He taught men so emphatically to revere tradition (Mt. xxiii.2) also recognised that this other situation could arise (Lk. xiv.26). How could there have been a Reformation unless this had been so? But when all this has been said the fearful warning of the story of Absalom, and the vehement words of the book of Proverbs, must be listened to by every generation. "The eye that mocketh at his father and despiseth to obey his mother, the ravens of the valley shall pluck it out and the young eagles shall eat it" (Prov. xxx.17).

4. The illumination of family life by the promise

God's purpose in calling the children of Israel to serve Him, in giving them the promise, and in setting their history in motion, is universal, even cosmic in its significance. It is to bring all human life back to its true nature and form, and to reveal again its true meaning.

We must admit that, for multitudes, life has entirely lost all meaning. What does it mean to be a man or a woman, to be a father or a son, a daughter or a mother? What does it mean to be married? The answers to such questions are beyond men. Somehow or other, nature by itself does not teach us its own meaning. Merely letting nature teach us what fatherhood means, what sonship means, or what marriage means, leads to a distortion of nature. When we try to be truly natural we often fail to be natural at all. And here all have failed and come short.

It is here, at the heart of this failure and distortion of human life, that God is beginning His restoring work in Israel, in order that, through what He does and reveals in Israel, the truth about nature and about human life may come to all nations. Within the sphere of His work in Israel God is going to allow a light to shine upon all family relationships, especially the parent-child, and the husband-wife relationship, that is going to illumine their meaning for all men in every age. This is what the Apostle Paul means when he writes to the Ephesians, and speaks of God as "The Father of our Lord Jesus Christ, of whom all fatherhood in heaven and earth is named" (Eph. III.14–15).

As God, in the land of Canaan, gradually fulfilled His promises to Israel, He was seeking to say first to this nation, and through this nation to the whole world, "I am the Father, the Father of my dear Son who is going to be born in your midst, The Father of my people, the Father of the individual, the Father of all; and when you see Him in the flesh acting as my Son and showing forth my Fatherhood as I too show it forth in Him, you will come to understand what all Fatherhood was made to image forth." This is the sum and substance of what He wanted to say about Himself to Israel. He is going to say this finally in the birth, life, and death and resurrection of Jesus. Through seeing Jesus, His people are to begin to understand what it means to have a heavenly Father, and thus come to understand earthly fatherhood. As God revealed Himself to Israel and as that revelation was gradually understood in its fulness, it was meant to illuminate at every level, the meaning of our intimate family relationships.

We must seek, then, to understand and pattern our family life within the Church on what we find in the Gospel. Here nature must find itself constantly challenged by grace. Since this light now shines upon earthly fatherhood, all the decisions we make within family relationships must now also show a difference. As children, we can no longer decide to judge parents only by what they are in themselves. We must now see them in this light, and honour them in this light. As parents, we must act as those who stand in this light, in all humility, and yet with new responsibility. The light shines on us whether we yield to it or not, but we must seek to pattern our whole family life on it; parents mirroring the strong faithfulness, love, justice, grace of the Father, against which children can mirror the freedom, faithfulness and obedience of Jesus Christ in His Sonship; children yielding to parents the trust and honour against the background of which the parents themselves are bound to come to an even deeper sense of their responsibility.

5. The illumination of the promise by family life

If family life is illuminated by, and patterned on, the promise, a miracle can take place. Nature, under the healing power of grace can become a witness to grace. Our earthly fatherhood and motherhood can bear witness to the divine light that shines on them through the Gospel and can be the means by which men come to understand God better.

One of the most striking facts of the Gospel is that Jesus could come into the midst of the life of his nation, and in spite of the sin and distortions of true humanity of which its life was full, He could speak to them about God being the "heavenly Father," knowing that here through centuries of good tradition and training under the light of God's grace, the word "Father" in itself had come to mean something rich and great. He could take even the ordinary emotions and experiences of fatherhood within the context of the life of the people, and could say, "if you feel like that about it, how much more so, does God feel!" "If a son shall ask bread of any of you that is a father, will he give him a stone? or if he ask a fish, will he for a fish give him a serpent? or if he ask an egg will he give him a scorpion? If ye then, being evil, know how to give good gifts unto your children: how much more shall your heavenly Father give the Holy Spirit to them that ask him?" (Lk. xi.11–13). Here, then, through centuries of patient long-suffering, of nurture in a tradition inspired by His grace, God can begin to tell Israel to look at what it has already been given within the gift of its family life, protected through this Commandment, and to see within it signs that point to the image in which He has made men like Himself. The meaning of His promise is illuminated by the light of His own grace shining within family life.

We know that it is a miracle of God's grace and love that this can happen at all. We know well that earthly fatherhood can take on so deformed a shape that it does nothing but distort the image of God. Then the word "father" comes to mean something debased—something to be shunned and feared. We know that earthly sonship can also easily lose the rich and true meaning it was meant to contain. And yet God in fulfilling His purposes, has overcome even such distortions.

And now through Christ His Son, God has given earthly fatherhood the power to reflect His own Fatherhood and earthly family life, the power to reflect the eternal relationships into accord with which He wants to restore human life.

"Before I had children of my own" wrote a great Christian, "I used to think, God will not forget me; but when I became a father I learned something more—God cannot forget me." It is only by grace, and not by nature, that men can say such things. A few years ago, a theological book was published with a dedication "To the little country Church rising from the open prairie, or the rocky shore-line, from the moorland, or the crown of the hill, and to that friendly company of fellow worshippers accustomed to gather Sabbath by Sabbath, among whom I see, through the mist of the years, the faces of my father and mother and many of the simple hearted saints of the earth." There is a deeper connexion than we sometimes imagine between the centuries of family worship Sabbath by Sabbath under the grace and commandment of the living God, and the ability to convey even such a dim reflexion of the divine life from one generation to another.

THE SIXTH COMMANDMENT

Exodus xx.13. *Thou shalt not kill.*

CHAPTER IX

THE FREEDOM TO LIVE

1. The cosmic goal and significance of the redeeming work of God

U P till now, the Commandments could easily have been read as if they were God's special word about a work He was going to do for a special people, with a limited end in view. It is only in the light of what finally happened in Jesus Christ, and its relevance for the whole world, that so far we have been able to see the significance for all mankind of the call to Israel to keep themselves separate from all other nations, to deny themselves rigidly in their use of imagery, to honour one particular divine personal name, to submit to being led under the protecting and chastening hand of God to a particular land, to sanctify one day in seven in rather a strange and demanding way. But now in the Sixth Commandment it suddenly becomes clear that the purpose and programme behind the bringing out of the Children of Israel from Egypt, and behind the giving of the first five Commandments, is to involve and embrace the whole of creation. In bringing Israel out of Egypt God is not merely saving one particular nation from a great and tragic predicament, but is starting a movement that must not cease till all life is saved from contempt or destruction. When God goes into action in Egypt and in the Red Sea, His purpose is not merely to set a handful of Semitic tribes free from their cruel taskmasters, but to redeem the whole creation from the distortions and murderous conflicts into which it has been plunged through the fall into sin, and to bring to fulfilment the truest aspiration of everything that feels pain and grasps after life. God wants to free everything from the threat of death which hangs so tragically over it. We find the promise of all this hidden here at the heart of the Ten Commandments.

1. East

2. The promise of life for all

"Thou shalt not kill." In this word, God says "Yes" to all life and to all creation. Here is His denial that the bloodshed, cruelty, and deadly warfare, that seem to be so deeply rooted in the natural life of the jungle and the forest, is His original design for life in this universe. Here, He throws His protecting arm round whatever lives and moves, and says, "This is Mine, and it is My will to save it from perishing!"

In their moments of insight, the great teachers of Israel realised that God's redeeming purpose had this cosmic reference. At times they were able to prophesy of the day when all the pain and conflict which had distorted and troubled nature would be abolished. When the prophet Isaiah had a vision of the captive Jews finally delivered from the Babylonian oppressors, making their way homewards through the deserts to Jerusalem, there to restore their national life and renew their service of God, he saw the trees of the field clapping their hands to encourage them on their journey, the briars replaced by myrtles, and the thorns replaced by fir trees, as nature looked on and understood something of the great things God was doing, and was going to do for her too, in Jerusalem (Is. LV.12–13). And in the final day, when God's purpose with Israel is consummated, the wolf is going to dwell with the lamb and the leopard lie down with the kid, "and the lion shall eat straw like the ox . . . they shall not hurt nor destroy in all my holy mountain: for the earth shall be full of the knowledge of the Lord, as the waters cover the sea" (Is. XI.5–9). To the prophets of Israel, the Lord they were serving was One whose call to men is always to turn from death, in order to live (Ezek. XVIII.33; XXXIII.11). The death from whose jaws they had been snatched when they were saved from the Red Sea, was something as evil as Pharaoh King of Egypt. The God who had destroyed Pharaoh was also going to destroy death. Therefore His people must never now assist the evil work of death in deliberately blighting human or animal life, or in increasing the corruption, pain, and distortion already in the heart of God's good creation—"Thou shalt not kill!"

Though all this is largely hidden in the Old Testament

Commandment, it is made perfectly clear when we come to the New Testament. Here we are shown that in Christ God has said, "Yes!" (II Cor. 1.19–20) to this earth and its life. God has not decreed the end of any life, but only the end of death, nothingness, and vanity. Though this world has taken a decisive turn, through its own absurd decision, towards such death and destruction, though it has become sick and evil, and has deserved the condemnation of death, God has not allowed death to have the last word, and has said again to His perishing creation, "Live!" He has so loved the world as to give His only begotten Son, not to condemn the world, but that the world through Him might have life (Jn. III.14–17). In raising Jesus from the dead as the "first fruits" of a new creation in which there shall be no more death nor sorrow nor pain, He has spoken clearly this final decisive word of life to everything under bondage of death (I Cor. xv.19–22, 54–7).

3. The murderous world

God's Word of life and resurrection has been spoken in the midst of a murderous world. We have to interpret this Commandment, therefore, not only in the light of the Resurrection of Jesus, but also against the background of the death of Jesus.

Jesus Christ came "that men might have life, and that they might have it more abundantly" (Jn. x.10). But this "Prince of life" (Acts III.15) was killed at the hands of men. The world which He came to save refused to receive Him, and, in a united, determined, and public way, arranged for Him to be put to death. Those responsible for His death were not the "killer type." They were ordinary people whom we would never dream of associating with any possible murder charge under normal social conditions.

This Commandment is therefore relevant for the ordinary people of every age who tend to indulge thoughtlessly and instinctively in the same kind of behaviour as made Jesus the victim of its killing. It is certainly also relevant for those who are being tempted to take physical vengeance into their own hands, and for thugs who go about with flick knives and knuckle dusters intent on creating social disturbances, and for the thieves who carry firearms when they do their housebreaking jobs, and for those who tend to go into fits of uncontrollably violent behaviour. But in its pressing urgency it is addressed to a much wider circle than such categories could cover. Indeed, it is addressed to the whole people of God in the midst of their daily pursuits. "All murders" says a recent writer on the Commandments, "converge and culminate in the crucifixion of Christ." In writing this he includes in the category of "murder" the official and private behaviour of all who within Church and State give way to anger or lack of love.

The modern problem of "death on the roads" is making us painfully aware of the way in which carelessness, recklessness, drink, and selfishness can kill even without any directly murderous intention. But the same characteristics of our behaviour have no less murderous consequences within other spheres of life. The exploitation of the homeless and unprotected in the direct satisfaction of sex lust and for commercial ends, can leave, in the end, a trail of helpless victims whose verdict on themselves might be, "better dead." The popular demand for entertainment on the lowest level that human morbidity or sadism can sink to, can degrade those who perform for it to a level in which all decency is destroyed, every good instinct crushed, and outrageous violence done to the image of God in which man was made. This, too, is killing. The ruthless pursuit of the profit motive through investment in enterprises where labour conditions bring about a quick wastage of human life can also bring responsibility for death to those who are all unconscious of the havoc that their wealth is being devoted to. The carelessness, or deliberate neglect, on the part of a technician or an engineer in a job in which public safety is involved, can lead to death on road, on rail, in air, or on the sea. If even in Old Testament times they counted a man guilty of death caused by faulty design in house roofs (Deut. xxii.8), or by failing to put guards round the verge of pits or wells (Ex. xxi.34 ff.) much more is to be expected of us today in our care for the safety of other members of the public.

"Out of the heart proceed . . . murders," Jesus said (Mt. xv.19), and when we try to qualify this very strong statement by asking which particular type of human heart is the

murderous type, we find that no qualification is possible. In
these words we are all included and all condemned. "Whence
come wars and fightings among you? Come they not hence
even from your lusts that war in your members? Ye lust and
have not: ye kill and desire to have and cannot obtain," writes
James (Jas. IV.1–2). He is writing simply to a group of early
Christians. Several things are obvious when we read the typical
story of the murder of Abel by Cain his brother. Cain was not a
specially depraved type, but simply a man living in the heart
of an ordinary family. What makes the difference between him
and Abel, is that he is not reconciled to God, and it is the
hatred in his heart to God that transfers itself to Abel and in the
course of its unrestrained expression gives rise to human murder (Gen. IV.3–8). This is why Jesus warned us that if we have
anger in our heart we are in danger of the judgment that
should fall on those who kill (Mt. V.21–2). "He that hateth his
brother is a murderer" (Jn. III.15).

4. A call to continual repentance

It would have saved us a good deal of heart-searching and
controversial ethical discussion if the Commandment, "Thou
shalt not kill," had a few qualifications attached to it, such as
"except when attacked under circumstances of war," or
"except in the case of the dangerous criminal murderer."
But there are no such qualifications. Indeed, it is impossible
that there should be any such. The promise hidden in the
Commandment is as universal as the scope of the death and
resurrection of Jesus Christ. It seeks to embrace all men, however unworthy, however criminal, however dangerous. Therefore the Commandment must read simply, "Thou shalt not
kill." The fact that such an unqualified command is spoken
to such an obviously murderous world must, surely, be meant
to disturb us deeply and to force us to re-think our accepted
practice.

Our accepted practice includes killing under certain circumstances. We kill the murderer. We kill in war. Our accepted way of thinking easily justifies this. We can appeal to
the clear words of Paul in Romans XIII, about the ruler having

the power of the sword from God in order to be a terror to the evil doer. There is our Confession of Faith with its unqualified assertion that under the New Testament the civil magistrate may wage war "upon just and necessary occasions". We can add further arguments from common sense. Are there not enemies who, if we do not kill them first, will kill us instead, and in killing us will destroy everything we have loved and lived for? And are there not crimes so revolting and terrible that justice could never be satisfied unless their perpetrators are known by an outraged society to have been hanged before satisfied witnesses?

We must constantly ask ourselves if such assertions and arguments are right. Whatever we do in the way of killing must be justified in the face of this unqualified Commandment, understood in the light of the death and resurrection of Jesus Christ. Spoken by God to a world in which killing is a practice deeply rooted in human nature, and in which war and capital punishment are too readily justified on the grounds of both morality and public order, it is obviously meant to throw men into tension and to create disturbing questions. The world in which those questions and controversies were not raised or taken with the utmost seriousness, would be a world in which the Word of God was not listened to at all.

The Commandment can be heard as an appeal to leave the vindication of justice ultimately in the hands of God. Certainly we must recognise that God has to a very large extent, put the vindication of earthly justice and the power to settle human disputes into the hands of earthly governments, judges, lawyers, and police. Yet nothing can alter the fact that through the death and resurrection of Jesus, God is both "just and the justifier of him which believeth in Jesus" (Rom. III.26). Enough has been done in this one death to satisfy justice and to declare God's righteousness, in the face of all human crime (Rom. III.25). Therefore we need no longer seek to justify capital punishment by talking about an outraged justice which still requires the death of the murderer. The question as to whether or not capital punishment deters the potential murderer and thus helps to guarantee public safety, remains very acute. But we are all involved so much in communal guilt that we require to have very powerful and clear arguments in favour of killing our criminal, and we would have to be convinced that our call for his death indeed arose out of justifiable argument, and was not the expression of something rather unworthy within ourselves.

Besides the question of the ultimate vindication of justice, there is the question of the ultimate vindication of earthly human rights, and the ultimate protection of human life over against the threat of possible chaos and universal destruction resulting from our manufacture of nuclear weapons. If we are justified in leaving the solution of the former question in the hands of the God and Father who led Jesus to the Cross, are we not also justified in leaving the solution of the latter question in the same hands which also raised Him from the dead?

Because Christ has died and risen, a Christian can never now talk as if war were inevitable, or as if the part which a Christian might play in a modern nuclear war were ever theoretically justifiable. War is to be regarded as possible only when all the sensible pacifistic arguments and alternatives have themselves proved untenable and impossible. In the actual situation which faces us today, pacifism even in its extreme forms must be regarded not simply as a prophetic protest against the ways of the world but as offering, even in extremely critical circumstances, a practical policy as safe as that of militarism.

Whatever we decide and do must be the outcome not of fear, but of faith in Jesus Christ. It must not therefore arise from a primary and blind trust in force. Force may be at times a useful instrument in the hands of faith. But even a club leader, or a parent, or a schoolteacher, has to learn that while force can sometimes achieve good ends, there is a point beyond which its use is not only futile but inevitably destructive of what we are seeking to achieve with it. The situation that faces us in the field of international relationships seems to have reached this point. The arguments that brought the Churches so convincedly to the support of governments in 1914 and 1939 have to be revised in the light of an immediate situation that calls on us to prove our willingness to repent, by our willingness to listen afresh to what this Commandment has to say to us in the midst of it.

5. The protection of life

Life in this world, as we have seen, is in many of its aspects like life in the jungle. In a multitude of spheres there are the same differences in the power to survive, the same pitiless life-or-death struggle, the same tragic fate for those who are weak. The law of the jungle too often prevails.

But the intrusion of the Kingdom of God already into the midst of this world's life in Jesus Christ is bound to produce even now, wherever His Gospel prevails, a reversal of this whole state of affairs. Paul, in his early days, found that even in one of his Churches they were behaving one to another exactly like the beasts of the forest, hounding each other down, tearing at each other's reputations, mercilessly, especially when the other man was exposed and defenceless. "If ye bite and devour one another," he wrote to them, "take heed that ye be not consumed one of another" (Gal. v.15). And then as he went on in his letter, he showed them the new law which, in contrast to the law of the jungle, must now be allowed to prevail amongst men. "Bear ye one another's burdens, and so fulfil the law of Christ" (Gal. vi.2).

Paul in this positive interpretation of the Commandment is obviously thinking of every type of burden. He is reminding us of our responsibility for relieving the human distress of all who are in danger of perishing, be it from hunger or poverty or accident or disease. We incur mortal responsibility when we possess the means to relieve mortal danger, however it is caused. We cannot escape the implications of the fact that Jesus Christ, who alone of all men was not responsible for any human guilt or suffering or need, took upon His heart the whole responsibility, in His free and glad acceptance of The Cross, and thereby left us an example.

This duty to relieve men of the crushing burdens of life, is often given by Paul a particular application to temptations which sometimes prove unsupportable to some men. Under the common burden of temptation borne by members of a social group some prove to be "strong" while others prove to be "weak." One Christian in Corinth, for instance, in the midst of a certain social situation in the company of other

Christians, found that what others were doing was a temptation to him to do what his conscience told him was wrong. But he was too weak to resist. Another, "stronger" Christian found no twinge of conscience at all either in the situation or in the indulgence. Paul, in this case had no hesitation in appealing to the "strong" to care for the "weak," as if it were a matter of life-or-death to his weak brother. The "weak" must not be emboldened by the example of the "strong" to violate conscience and court perdition. The "strong" must not "destroy" by his casual and careless behaviour a "brother for whom Christ died" (Rom. xiv.15; 1 Cor. viii.11). "We, then, that are strong ought to bear the infirmities of the weak, and not to please ourselves" (Rom. xv.1).

The Church is often blamed for talking too much about the dangers lurking round alcohol, sex, and gambling, but it is with relation to these that far too many of us show ourselves "weak" either in conscience or in power to resist, and no one can deny that casualties of tragic nature result when men violate their conscience in such matters, and cease to have either any reference by which to guide themselves or any power by which to control themselves. "Jesus Christ" said Phillips Brooks, "came to assert the rights of the weak over the strong as part of the moral structure of the universe."

We cannot, in theory, set any limit to the command to protect human life from death. Time and again under tragic circumstances we are asked to consider the real possibility, for instance, of terminating the life of an unborn child when otherwise the mother's life is seriously endangered during its birth, or of killing the foetus of a future baby likely to be born deformed, or of putting an end to the life of someone suffering from a painful, protracted and incurable disease, or of justifying suicide, for instance, by a woman threatened with rape, or by a politician who fears that he might be forced by torture to betray his country. In many such cases it seems impossible to concede to any human being, or group of human beings, the right to decide when a life is so worthless in the sight of God that it must now be deliberately exterminated or to choose beforehand between two human beings the one that must be preferred for survival even when death threatens both. It may

be that in the midst of the latter situation a clear guidance will
be given to those who have to accept responsibility for the care
of it. Generally speaking, life must be protected from death.
But even in saying this, we cannot exclude the possibility that
no such general rule is adequate in face of other factors that
might unforseeably claim a consideration prior to that of the
protection of life.

6. Claiming the promise

This is not merely a command to "let live." It is also a
command to "live." It challenges us to use, possess and enjoy
all the good and beautiful things of life which God puts at our
disposal in this earth. God has made many things beautiful,
interesting, and enjoyable for man even in his bodily, earthly,
life. Human culture, in its most basic and true forms, arises out
of His inspiration and endowment, even of sinful men. We
must take seriously the fact that the "Yes" He has spoken in
Christ, is more emphatic and decisive than any "No" that He
has spoken even in the exercise of His judgments.

We must frankly recognise the limitations that have been set
in the way of an enjoyment of life. The purest earthly joys have
a rather frustrating element of transitoriness (Eccl. 1, 11).
Their unrestrained pursuit can hinder our response to the
Kingdom of God, and can only too easily involve us in compromise with evil. Nevertheless, in our attitude to life, and
what it offers us, we must not give way to daemonic suggestions
that inspire cynicism and gloom, and seek to blight our enjoyment of what God has called "good." We must listen again to
the positive commands scattered throughout Holy Scripture
that call us to rejoice in all that God has given us under the
sun. It is precisely in the Book of Ecclesiastes where we find a
man under the Word of God trying to face frankly up to the
havoc wrought by the element of vanity and evil within this
good creation, that we find time and again this call to live.
"Behold that which I have seen: it is good and comely for one
to eat and to drink, and to enjoy the good of all his labour that
he taketh under the sun all the days of his life which God
giveth him, for it is his portion. Every man also to whom God

hath given riches and wealth, and hath given him power to eat thereof and to take his portion and to rejoice in his labour; this is the gift of God" (Eccl. v.18–19; cp. ix.7–10; xi.9).

If we listen to the words of this Commandment as a challenge to live positively in the light of the resurrection of Jesus, we are more likely to recognise the sinister nature of the temptation to suicide. This is a temptation not only to usurp God's right to dispose of the life He has given to us, and to make a tragic abuse of the gift of our human freedom, but also to reject in sheer unbelief the gift of life which God holds out anew to all men, and especially to the despairing, in Jesus Christ.

The Commandment, further, calls from us a "reverence for life" in all its true forms as far as we can know these. If we live under its challenge, we are bound to hate the things which destroy, maim, or abuse the fair form which He has given both to man's life and to his living environment. For instance, the Bible suggests that it is only through a tragic necessity that man has been forced to kill animal life for his food. It is because of his absurd and disastrous refusal to live in a true relationship with God that he can no longer live in a true relationship with his creaturely environment, for the "curse" (Gen. iii.17–21) that has blighted man's own life has also disturbed and blighted the life of the dumb creation which now "groaneth and travaileth in pain" waiting for the day when it will share in the "glorious liberty" of man's redemption (Rom. viii.19–22). If man understands this, will he not understand that the command, "Thou shalt not kill" also has some reference to his killing of animal life? If we must kill for food, need we find any pleasure in the process of killing, and need we indulge in unnecessary killing? Can blood-sport really become the pastime of a Christian? There are certainly also false and distorted forms of creaturely life around us that we have to destroy if we are to live and defend what seems to us, in the light of Christ, to be good. If in such cases we have to kill, we must do so in repentance and faith, looking for the day "when the creature itself shall be delivered from the bondage of corruption" (Rom. viii.21).

THE SEVENTH COMMANDMENT

EXODUS xx. 14. *Thou shalt not commit adultery.*

CHAPTER X

THE IMAGE OF GOD IN MARRIED LOVE

1. The Gospel of Christ and the meaning of marriage

THE story of God's relationship to the people of Israel had a certain amount of romance about it. His heart was moved with pity for them where He saw them suffering under cruel bondage in Egypt. In rescuing them from their captivity, He never failed to stand Himself beside them in love, speaking to them a personal word. He entered a solemn covenant with them to be their God for ever, promising that they, too, should be His people for ever.

As the great Prophets of Israel looked back upon the early history of Israel from a later standpoint this element of romance loomed very large (Jer. II.1–3; Hos. XI.1–4). It seemed to them that the whole affair could be described as the story of a marriage, for all the elements that are required for a true human marriage seemed to be there. There was the free choice of the bride by the bridegroom, and the wooing of her with deeds and words of love. There was the free choice on the part of the bride, for, in spite of the disobedience and hardness of heart which Israel often showed, there were times of true response, and there were individuals who in the name of their whole nation could break out into the language of passionate and ardent devotion to Him who sought them: "O God, thou art my God; early will I seek thee: my soul thirsteth for thee, my flesh longeth for thee" (Ps. LXIII.1); "Lord, thou hast searched me, and known me. Thou knowest my downsitting and mine uprising, thou understandest my thought afar off" (Ps. CXXXIX.1–2). There was the solemn covenant, pledging unbreakable faithfulness and lasting love, entered into with fitting ceremony and uttered vows (Ex. XXIV). There were the visible pledges and signs, like the wedding ring, given to each other by both bridegroom and bride. God on His side gave Israel signs such as the passover feast, reminding them of God's pledge to be with them. Israel on her side set up here and there throughout the land stone pillars and monuments as perpetual signs that she had chosen and pledged herself to be the Lord's. There was the life together in which God more and more became identified with Israel, shared her afflictions and sorrows, and bore the burden, and even the shame, of the relationship which He had entered with her. Israel was married to God, and God to Israel (Jer. III.14; Is. LIV, LXII.4).

Of course there are features in the whole story which do not fit into the pattern of ordinary human marriage. Never could there be such a one-sided marriage in human life as this! Here the whole initiative was taken by God and the whole burden was borne by God. The other party to the wedding was more unfaithful, and more often forgiven, than would be possible in any human marriage. Yet the analogy remains, in spite of such distorting features. One of the truest descriptions of the whole purpose behind God's dealings with His people in the Old Testament is given by Hosea, when in face of the unfaithfulness that he well knows, he passes on God's unchangeable promise to His people. "And I will betroth thee unto me for ever; yea I will betroth thee unto me in righteousness and in judgment and in loving kindness, and in mercies. I will even betroth thee unto me in faithfulness, and thou shalt know the Lord" (Hos. II.19–20). To the relationship set up between God and His people, even though so often vitiated by sin and unfaithfulness on the part of Israel, in its intimacy, power, and indissolubility the nearest thing on earth that corresponds to it is true marriage.

What God sought to do and to be to Israel, is brought to its climax and fulfilment in the relationship established between Christ and the Church in the New Testament. In the prologue to the Gospel of John we have this put in quite blunt and realistic language: "In the beginning was the Word, and the Word was with God, and the Word was God. . . . And the Word was made flesh and dwelt amongst us" (Jn. I.1, 14). Here is the assertion that in the person of Jesus, God has entered into a union with men so close that, as in marriage, the two are "one flesh." In the Gospels, Jesus describes Himself as the "Bridegroom" of His people. He speaks and acts as the One who has come to re-enact towards His new community, the Church, the whole drama of God's love for Israel as shown in the Old Testament. His calling of the disciples, His self-giving to them in friendship and love, His patience with them in their unfaithfulness, misunderstanding, and stubbornness, His sighs over them, His pleading with them, His prayers for them, His constant watchfulness over their safety, all recall, often in very striking detail, the story of God and His people Israel. Before Jesus finally left His disciples, He enacted with them a solemn ceremony in the context of a Passover meal, which emphasised both the intimate unity of "one flesh" into which it was His purpose to bring them in relation to Himself, and the inviolate covenant that must establish and guard this unity. He took bread and blessed and "brake it, and said, Take eat: this is my body which is broken for you: this do in remembrance of me. After the same manner also he took the cup, saying: This cup is the new testament in my blood: This do ye, as oft as ye drink it, in remembrance of me" (1 Cor. XI.24–5).

In Jesus, then, we have God entering a union with man so intimate, enduring, and indissoluble, that we are not surprised to find in many places in the New Testament the language of marriage used to describe it (Jn. III.29; Mt. IX.15; Rev. IX.7, XXI.2). It is, moreover, primarily at the Lord's Table that we realise that marriage is the human relationship that is most adequate to convey the power and love and reality of this new closeness of God to man. It is with such a thought in his mind that Paul describes conversion from heathenism to Christianity as "espousal to Christ" (II Cor. XI.2), and encourages his readers to live in conformity to the Gospel, especially in matters involving sex, by reminding them that through what God has done for them by bringing them to faith in Jesus, they are united in body and soul to the Lord, and that therefore their members are the members of Christ (1 Cor. VI.13–20). It is significant that it is when Paul is seeking to drive home to husbands and wives the true nature of their relationship one with another, that he again returns to the relationship of Christ to the Church, and holds this up, in its intimacy and fulness, as the example of what a true marriage should hold in its heart. "Husbands, love your wives, even as Christ also loved the church, and gave Himself for it; that He might sanctify and cleanse it, with the washing of water by the word. That He might present it to himself a glorious church, not having spot, or wrinkle, or any such thing; but that it should be holy and without blemish" (Eph. v.25–6).

This union between Christ and His Church, like that between God and Israel, is based on the forgiveness of the sins of the bride by the Bridegroom. The marriage is possible only through the faithful, patient and completely self-sacrificing love of Christ who constantly cleanses, restores and holds on to it, with a love that "suffereth long and is kind; . . . envieth not; . . . vaunteth not itself, is not puffed up, doth not behave itself unseemly, seeketh not her own, is not easily provoked, thinketh no evil; rejoiceth not in iniquity, but rejoiceth in the truth; beareth all things, believeth all things, hopeth all things, endureth all things" (1 Cor. xiii.4–7). Even in the one-sidedness of this love, we have an example of the love that from both sides must be the basis of true marriage between man and wife.

2. The healing and restoration of the marriage relationship by Jesus Christ

Jesus Christ came to earth not only to reveal the true pattern of the marriage relationship, but also to make it possible by His presence and blessing in the midst of human life, for ordinary men and women to enter such a true marriage relationship. As we have already seen (pp. 102–3), the purpose for which Jesus came into the world, and the end to which His whole life's work was directed, was to restore human life and the whole natural creation to what God meant it to be when He created it. Through man's original sin, and constant wrong-doing, everything in human life and nature has become full of distortions, diseases, and inadequacies that were never meant to be there when "in the beginning God created the heaven and the earth" (Gen. 1.1) and made all things "good" (Gen. 1.4; Eccl. iii.11). Jesus has come to redeem the whole world from this chaos, ugliness, and distortion.

It is especially in the relationships between God and man, and between one man and another within community, and family life, that Jesus has begun His redeeming and restoring work. Even of Jesus' forerunner, John the Baptist, it was prophesied that he would "turn the heart of the fathers to the children, and the heart of the children to their fathers" (Mal. IV.6). In recording the raising of the widow's son at Nain, Luke closes his narrative with the words "and he delivered him to his mother" (Lk. XI.15), and after his account of the cure of the epileptic child he notes that Jesus "delivered him again to his father" (Lk. IX.42). It is likely that Luke had a double meaning in his use of such phrases in his witness to the Christ.

In coming to rescue and restore human relationships to their true nature, Jesus was especially concerned about marriage. In His teaching about it, He by-passed the Old Testament examples and laws, some of which to His mind reflected only a distorted and corrupted form of marriage, and sought to take men back to the meaning which marriage had "in the beginning" for all mankind in the purpose of God (cp. Mt. XIX.7–8). He went back to the story of creation in the early chapters of Genesis: "And the Lord God said, it is not good that the man should be alone; I will make an help meet for him. . . . And the Lord God caused a deep sleep to fall upon Adam, and he slept: and he took one of his ribs and closed up the flesh instead thereof; and the rib which the Lord God had taken from the man made he a woman; and brought her unto the man. And Adam said, this is now bone of my bones and flesh of my flesh: she shall be called woman, for she was taken out of Man" (Gen. II.18, 21–23). But He not only directed men's minds to what was "in the beginning," He also made it possible for men and women here and now, in His presence, to enter into such a true marriage relationship.

Early in His ministry Jesus gave a sign that human marriage was going to be vitally affected for good by the work He was going to begin on earth for the "restoration of all things," (Acts III.21). He was invited as a guest to a wedding at Cana in Galilee (Jn. II). He was in no way prominent amongst the guests. Indeed the whole of the time He kept in the background, and few were conscious that He was there at all. But when a crisis occurred and the joy and success of the day, and indeed of the marriage, were threatened by the running out of what was regarded as a most vital element in the celebration, the wine, then, all unknown and unacknowledged either by the host of the feast or by the bride and bridegroom concerned, Jesus saved the deteriorating human situation and restored the vitality and joy that was tending to run out both of the social occasion and what it signified. All this is a sign that even though He remains in the background of human life, Jesus' presence in the world, in His hidden work in upholding and restoring creation, constantly saves what is growing insipid and meaningless from the vanity and emptiness that is bound to characterise life apart from Him, and that was experienced in Old Testament times even by those who believed in God (cp. Eccl. I, II). This especially applies to marriage, to which He has come to give real meaning and stability wherever in human life His presence is accepted.

3. The essential implications of a marriage

(i) Gift

Marriage involves the glad and simple acceptance of a special gift bestowed on two individuals chosen for each other, and choosing each other in the light of the fact that they believe themselves thus chosen.

After Jesus took His disciples back to the Old Testament story of the creation of Eve for Adam "in the beginning," and the giving of each to the other as specially destined for each other, he quoted the saying about marriage which concludes that story, "For this cause shall a man leave his father and mother, and cleave to his wife; and they twain shall be one flesh: so then they are no more twain, but one flesh" (Mk. x.9). Did He not intend them to look on this element of choosing under a sense of being chosen, as an important part of every marriage? Now they cannot possibly think of marriage as involving anything other than one man and one woman to the exclusion and forsaking of all others. To cleave to one is to let go of another. This also corresponds with the simple fact that God has only one Israel, and Christ has only one Church. In the light of this fact the beautiful stories of Isaac and Rebekah (in spite of its rather sad developments), and of Jacob and Rachel (in spite of Leah), shine out as far more true to God's purpose for men and women than those of David's affairs with women, proving that even in Israel, in spite of its toleration of polygamy, there was a good deal of true insight. Many other aspects of married life also constitute arguments for monogamy, but this one seems to be decisive in itself.

The acceptance of this gift seems to imply that freedom of choice is an important element in a marriage that is true to the intention of God. The fact that successful marriages have in the past been arranged and forced on couples by social custom and pressure, or by parental domination is simply due to the fact that other aspects of the gift and the grace of God have at times been strong enough to overcome this primary distortion. But if we have come to a better understanding of this essential aspect of marriage we must not continue to tempt the grace of God by bringing further pressure to bear in the creation of marriages. It signifies real progress in our thinking in this subject to find many who write on it insisting on the importance of this aspect of marriage, and asserting that what is felt to be "forced" may not be marriage.

(ii) Task

Man and woman, are brought together by God and come together of their own free-will, in order to become "one flesh." Commentators on the Biblical texts which include this phrase are at pains to point out that though the phrase "one flesh" includes the sexual encounter and sharing, it includes it only as part, and not the main part, of a much wider sharing of self, possessions, and life-interest.

The "one flesh" marriage relationship of Christ to His Church involves primarily the closest identification of the Lord with His people throughout the whole course of their history. It includes the bestowal by Christ upon the Church of all His wealth, purity, glory, and strength, His constant bearing of its weakness and shame in a love that is anxiously concerned over every detail of its welfare. It involves the Church, in response, in making a total offering of all its devotion, possessions, and service in a confident gratitude that surrenders everything.

The implications of this analogy are well brought out by

Otto Piper. In marriage "the couple owe to each other all that they have and are, in the same way as is the case in the relationship between Christ and the Church. The Lord possesses nothing outside the Church, and the Church possesses nothing except her love for Him. The same holds good of the married pair. . . . Neither can say of himself that he possesses anything of his own; both have everything in common, not only goods, leisure and strength, but also joy and sorrow, hopes and fears. Hence marital life is not a mutual exchange of services, but a living fellowship in which each takes all that he has, or is able to do, and uses it for the benefit of the other, for the sake of the love of God. . . . Each would only rob the other if each gave the other less than his or her whole person in all its physical and mental aspects and all its social and economic implications" (*The Christian Interpretation of Sex*, 1st edn., pp. 163–4).

It is obvious that becoming "one flesh" in this sense is not something that simply "happens" when somehow a couple are "officially" married by Church or State, or when they come together in sexual intercourse. It is rather a task that has to be fulfilled involving decision, self-denial, growth into fulness of dedication. It involves, as Karl Barth puts it, a "labour at the work of art of their common being" (*Church Dogmatics*, VOL. III, PT. IV, p. 188), and it is worth while to quote from his fuller description of what this common life-partnership involves: "Marriage as a life-partnership is therefore the proof of love. In marriage as a life-partnership it is a matter of repeating in all seriousness the Yes of love. But 'in all seriousness' means in a life which is the whole life of man, in toil and care, in joy and pain, in sickness and health, in youth and age, in wrestling with the many questions, small and great, inner and outer, individual and social, which lovers united in a common life can and may as little evade as other men, but all these things in the fellowship of their life, in some way or other together, in the special orientation of the one on the other, in the evenness of step between the two selected and willed for this purpose. 'In all seriousness' means experiencing all this in the succession of unforeseeably many days of twenty-four hours and unforeseeably many years of fifty-two weeks, with the intimacy of an everyday and everynight companionship which discloses everything on both sides, in which each very soon gets to know the other with terrifying exactitude, and in which the greatest thing can become astonishingly small and the smallest astonishingly great. 'In all seriousness' means to have become a collective, a We, a pair, and to live as such, not merely outwardly but inwardly as the only possible basis of the outward, and not merely in the life of mutual relations, but in the thinking, willing, and feeling of both participants upon which these relations must rest if they are to be tenable" (*Church Dogmatics* VOL. III, PT. IV, p. 187).

Of course, just as the choosing of one by the other may include a basic element of "sex attraction," so the becoming "one flesh" includes a basic element of sexual intercourse. This may even be a powerful force in binding the two together in "one flesh," and Jesus may have had this particularly in mind when He quoted the words of Genesis about a man leaving father and mother and cleaving to his wife. To this extent "God has written the law of man's physical being within his spiritual nature." Just as the body is inseparable from the soul in the unity of soul and body, so sex intercourse is inseparable from the other elements which go to make up a true marriage union. Some writers can speak of the sex activity within marriage as having almost the virtue of a sacrament. "The sex instinct in the Bible," says Tournier, "is not a . . . vulgar accident but an element in God's scheme of things. By bringing man and woman together and making their encounter genuine communion in which each possesses the other body and soul, it leads to the discovery of the profoundest spiritual realities."

A much wider and fuller sharing, however, than that immediately involved in sex intercourse is necessary to the two becoming "one flesh." While man's or woman's sexuality is included and used, and thus sanctified by its use, in the becoming "one flesh" of husband and wife, it is nevertheless placed in a position of sheer subordination to the other elements, just as the body is subordinate to the soul in the unseparable unity of soul and body. "Sex" here is good, but it is good only in its proper place, at its proper time, and in its proper proportion. While sex can serve marriage, it would be a perversion indeed if marriage were thought of as made to serve sex. This particular point of encounter in marriage, as Barth, again, points out "should remain a point of transition, having its own weight and honour in the whole, but not breaking loose from the whole."

It will be obvious that if the attempt is made to divorce the sex intercourse from its service of the whole task of marriage, or unduly to emphasise its importance to the neglect of the other aspects of the marriage union, a serious distortion is made in the true form which marriage should be made to take. Sex now, instead of serving true love, becomes harnessed to man's self-centredness. Therefore sex instead of becoming a God-given means for furthering the true personal communion and self-giving at every level of life, becomes a means of essentially selfish satisfaction at the expense of the other partner. It thus tends to destroy the possibility of the very relationship it was designed to help and foster. Sex in this case can become essentially promiscuous even though it is indulged only within the legal marriage bonds.

It is in this light that we must judge the arguments, made today in many quarters, that in view of the long periods through which young couples are forced to wait before it is economically possible for them to settle down in officially married life, and the safeguards afforded by modern contraceptive devices, no condemnation should be pronounced and no prohibition placed on the practice of sex intercourse by couples who are engaged to be married, and seriously intend to enter a future life-partnership. Even some who would vigorously condemn promiscuous sex relations, would except such cases from the condemnation.

It does not seem difficult to answer such arguments. The insistence on a right to enter preliminary experimental sex intercourse before any determined and recognised attempt to embark on a complete life-partnership, would imply that sex had already broken loose from its proper place, had already thrust itself in front in a way that is destructive of the love which can alone be the basis of true marriage (cp. 1 Cor.xiii). It would imply that already, before marriage is entered, the ability of both partners for the real task together was deeply called in question, for the task of marriage for Christians involves in its day-by-day details as much as any other task, obedience to the call of Jesus Christ: "If any man will come after me, let him deny himself" (Mt. xvi.24). It would mean, too, that a serious decision had been made by both that the body was to be allowed to take the initiative over the soul. It would mean, too, an extremely bold and dubious reinterpretation of the teaching both of Jesus Himself and the New Testament. In our Lord's references to this aspect of moral behaviour there is not a hint that the definition of fornication could be narrowed down to exclude the cases under discussion, and its general practice is condemned in such an unqualified and positive manner as to indicate that here any borderline manœuvering is impossible.

(iii) Covenant

Though marriage, in its essentially inward nature, is a gift and a task that primarily concern two particular individuals, yet in its outward nature it cannot avoid taking the form of a public institution. If a man is to "leave father and mother" in order to cleave to his wife, he should do so with the public co-operation of both "father and mother" and society itself, all consenting to what cannot fail to be a public action of a very important nature. The State, the family, and Church should provide for this being done "decently and in order" (1 Cor. xiv.40).

Therefore, though marriages are made neither by Church or State, they must be acknowledged and protected by Church and State and respected by other men. It is obvious that this involves more than the mere conduct of marriage services by the Church, and the registration of marriage by the State. We have already seen that true marriage can be protected by certain moral conventions which make a true approach to it possible. Society should also afford it protection against any possible interference by some third party, and conditions created by society in the economic sphere, and in the sphere of housing, should make it possible for couples at a normally mature age to enter such life-partnership in the independence necessary to pursue married life.

Alongside such recognition and protection of marriage by

State, family, and Church, there must obviously be the willingness by those who accept such recognition and protection, to
enter some form of sworn mutual covenant under which they
bind themselves to their task together. We must remember that
Jesus, in bringing to light the nature of true marriage, lent His
unqualified approval to the custom of making public entry
into marriage a notable "occasion," giving His presence at the
wedding in Cana of Galilee in response to a normally sent
invitation (Jn. ii), and speaking about current customs relating
to public marriages as if these were good and healthy institutions (cp. Mt. xxii.4–14; xxv.1–13).

(iv) Fact

The acceptance of the gift and the task of marriage implies
the acceptance of an irreversible fact.

Jesus' words about marriage imply that when two are
brought together in marriage, as they seek to fulfil the life-task
before them, entering their union in all its aspects inward and
outward, they have to be regarded in the sight of God and by
an act of God as being actually "joined together" in such a real
way that henceforth the one can no longer be without the
other. A fact has taken place, based on the purpose of God in
creating man male and female (Gen. 1.27). Now they are like a
single being, or person, or organism which fulfils its place and
function in society only in its two-foldness, and which it is
impossible now to pull apart into two single significant pieces.
In the midst of their life in this union they reflect in a new way
in their togetherness, the image of God (cp. Gen. 1.27) "Wherefore," said Jesus, emphasising and commenting on the Genesis
account of the nature of marriage, "they are no more twain,
but one flesh. What therefore God hath joined together, let not
man put asunder" (Mt. xix.6).

How and when are we to think of this irreversible fact as
having been accomplished? From the Genesis quotation, which
Jesus found so significant, it might be concluded that the
becoming "one flesh" was coincident with the public act of a
man definitely breaking relations with his old home and setting
up a new family relationship with his wife. Therefore there is
basis for regarding the pronouncing of man and woman to be

husband and wife in a marriage ceremony as having significance in making them one.

There is also some basis for regarding the sex union itself as being, in the creative will of God, a means whereby the two parties become inseparably joined in "one flesh" and the irreversible fact of marriage is finally effected. This fact seems to be in Paul's mind when, writing to the Corinthians, he points out that indulgence in sex intercourse affects the parties engaged in it in quite a different way from indulgence in the appetites such as eating and drinking. Food affects only the "stomach" and God will destroy both one and the other he argues, but sex intercourse affects "the body" which is for the Lord, and which will be given a place in our ultimate resurrection in the likeness of Christ. At the present day our bodies being united to Christ are members of Christ. "Shall I take the members of Christ and make them members of an harlot? God forbid. What? Know ye not that he which is joined to an harlot is one body? for the two, saith he, shall be one flesh." (cp. 1 Cor. VI.13-20). It is obvious that he regards sex intercourse even without any other accompanying personal relationship, or fellowship, as in itself setting up through the creative ordinance of God certain bonds of a serious and deep nature between two parties. The fact of sex intercourse rightly used in marriage is therefore an important aspect of the bond of union.

But the union of sex, apart from the whole commitment to a life task and a public covenant, cannot be regarded as creating in itself such a stable union as to constitute a marriage bond. The irreversible union of "one flesh" must be regarded as a manifold and growing bond, both given by God on one side and achieved by the partners on the other side, in the midst of every aspect of their life together.

The irreversibility of this fact, as it must be assumed to take place in its manifold strength within every marriage union, makes us understand how impossible it is to dissolve a marriage by any legal enactment, or indeed any kind of human or ecclesiastical decision. When Jesus said "What, therefore God hath joined together let not man put asunder" (Mk. x.9), He was stating an impossibility rather than making a legal enactment. And His further judgment, "Whosoever shall put away his wife, and marry another, committeth adultery against her. And if a woman shall put away her husband, and be married to another, she committeth adultery" (Mk. x.11–12), is based on the same basic impossibility of thinking that divorce can really take place, since a marriage has become fact.

4. The further implications of the task

In its statement of the purposes for which marriage was given to man by God, the preamble to the marriage service as celebrated within the Church of Scotland mentions first of all that it "was ordained for the life-long companionship, help, and comfort, which husband and wife ought to have of each other". The preamble then proceeds: "It was ordained also for the continuance of the holy ordinance of family life, that children, who are the heritage of the Lord, should be duly nurtured and trained up in godliness."

The "task" undertaken in marriage is obviously meant, under normal circumstances, to include the rearing of children within family life. In marriage, God allows a man and a woman in their togetherness not only to reflect His image, but also to share in His creative activity in bringing new lives into being. Deliberately to refuse to share in this aspect of the gift of marriage would be deliberately to reject God's grace in the gift. Can any couple claim to be honestly sharing in the common task to which they are called in undertaking marriage, if they deliberately avoid becoming involved together in the responsibility for a full family life? Would they not, in such a case, be avoiding the providential burdens and privileges involved from the start in their calling, and in the midst of which they are meant to find their union one with another deepened and enriched?

Therefore when we define the ends for which marriage was ordained, the task of bearing and nurturing children must always be mentioned. In stressing this aspect of marriage, in its proper place, the essentially monogamous nature of marriage is clearly indicated. Indeed, from the simple facts involved in this aspect of the task of marriage, powerful natural arguments can be brought forward, underlining the other arguments for monogamy and chastity that are clearly implied in what the Gospel itself reveals about marriage.

But this aspect of the task of marriage should be stressed only after the essential nature of marriage has been discovered in the "help and comfort which husband and wife ought to have of each other." That which constitutes a real and full married life can be understood, defined, and satisfyingly experienced without the procreation of children. It seems to be in accordance with the general teaching of the Bible to stress the duty of child-bearing under the discussion of the fifth commandment, and simply to consider it in a secondary way in the discussion of the seventh commandment. It would tend to caricature marriage if a man were encouraged to choose a wife mainly for the purpose of having someone through whom to produce and rear a family. It would be equally undesirable for the Church, in its zeal to "be fruitful and multiply" in order to "subdue the earth" (Gen. 1.28), to emphasise so much the duty of producing large families that the real nature of the marriage relationship between husband and wife became obscured.

The claim of God's grace in both the fifth and seventh commandments forces Christians to make some decision about the use of contraceptive devices. It would be wrong for such use to be made without considering seriously the issues. On theological grounds cogent arguments can be given for their disciplined use. If God's creative activity is the expression both of His freedom and His deliberate planning, then it is arguable that freedom and deliberate planning are desirable elements to introduce into human procreative activity. If artificial means are used by man in disciplining the fruitfulness of the earth, then it seems logical that artificial means can also be used in disciplining the fruitfulness of the human race. Generally speaking, therefore, this is an issue in which the medical and humanitarian arguments can be allowed to weigh heavily in coming to a decision whether or not, in a particular situation, modern birth-control methods are to be recommended.

But obviously it would be unwise for the Church to lay down any general rule intended to be applicable to every situation. The question of the personal use of contraceptives within the marriage relationship is bound often to involve a discussion of cases so complicated as to be beyond the scope of simple rules. Such cases should come under the pastoral care of the Church rather than under its legal enactment. It is certain, however, that control of the distribution and use of contraceptives is as important a matter both for society and the individual as the control of alcohol and drugs. If contraceptives themselves are justified as a means of control, the logic of this must be thoroughly accepted.

CHAPTER XI

MARRIAGE, CHURCH, AND SOCIETY

1. An adulterous generation

THE generation to which Jesus brought such teaching on marriage as we have been discussing, and before which Jesus held out such possibilities in the sphere of marriage, was both uneasy in its whole attitude, and disordered in its behaviour, in matters of sex.

When the disciples heard from Jesus that marriage was of such a nature as to imply only one wife for one man, as to involve necessarily the submission of sex to the true love of one person, and the impossibility of divorce, they were completely bewildered. It had not dawned on them that Moses could have been compromising when he allowed divorce, or that a King like David in his marriage relationship with several wives should be thought of as indulging in something that was not the truest expression of the will of God for men. Jesus' words passed judgment on their traditional views of marriage. It is obvious that they had been brought up with such a view as enabled them to make easy allowance for polygamy, divorce, and sex licence. This view could be summarised in the recent definition

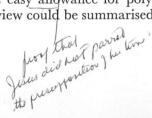

proof that Jesus did not pass the presupposition of his time

of marriage seriously given in a popular Bible Dictionary: "Marriage is a state in which men and women can live together in sexual relationship with the approval of their social group."

But now Jesus was proposing something quite new. His teaching made polygamy impossible, made divorce unthinkable, and took marriage entirely out of the sphere of licenced sex indulgence. Their uneasiness as they listened to Jesus must have been heightened by their memory of His words in the Sermon on the Mount, repeated probably on several occasions. "Ye have heard that it was said by them of old time, Thou shalt not commit adultery: But I say unto you, that whosoever looketh on a woman to lust after her hath committed adultery already with her in his heart" (Mt. v.28). They were too bewildered and disturbed in their minds to engage in public discussion with Jesus as He spoke about these matters, but as soon as they were in private, they put their perplexities to Him. "And in the house his disciples asked him again of the same matter" (Mk. x.10). Matthew tells us that after Jesus repeated to them His teaching about the impossibility of divorce, they expressed their astonishment in the words: "If the case of a man be so with his wife, it is not good to marry" (Mt. xix.10).

The same uneasy conscience in the presence of Jesus over their current affairs relating to sex was betrayed by the Pharisees, when they brought to Him the woman taken in the very act of adultery, seeking confirmation from Him for the verdict written in the law of Moses that she should be stoned. When they brought her into His presence Jesus remained silent, stooped, and wrote with His finger in the sand. (Did He write His words about adultery in the heart?) Then raising Himself, He said, "He that is without sin among you, let him first cast a stone at her." They could ask no more questions in His presence and "beginning at the eldest, even unto the last" they quitted His presence in silence and left the woman alone with Him (Jn. viii.1–10).

There is, of course, according to the teaching of the Bible, a reserve in certain aspects of the sex life that is healthy. The early chapters of Genesis on which our Lord based so much of His teaching on sex point to the sense of shame as a gift given by God's grace to men and women to enable them to face the

consequences of their human sinfulness and frailty (Gen.
III.7–12), and we can only conclude that the instinct to become
reserved in this way is due to the need for the protection of the
human body and the human personality from exploitation and
enslavement in this sphere. But there is a very great difference
between the deliberate reserve of faith within matters relating
to sex, and the uneasy conscience that is manifested by those
who were confronted by Jesus' teaching on the subject.

In view of all this it is obvious that when Jesus once addressed
the people of His day as an "evil and adulterous generation"
(Mt. XII.39), He was not speaking in a purely metaphorical
sense. The adjective "adulterous" fitted not simply their faithlessness in the sphere of religious loyalty, but their thoughts and
behaviour in the whole sphere of sex and marriage.

If the Jews, in the days of Jesus, were unhappy in their
attempts to order their affairs in the sphere of marriage and
sex, there is every sign that some of the Gentile communities
had lost all ability to control anything at all in this sphere.
Paul's stern and reasoned appeals to the Corinthians to be
guided in their sex behaviour by the Gospel are obviously
addressed to them against a background of pagan life in which
sex has broken loose from any vestige of true direction, and his
passing description of the homosexuality which must have been
well known to the readers of his epistle to the Romans is
another pointer to the same conclusion (Rom. 1.23–7).

Can any of us today escape the feeling that we, too, belong
to an adulterous generation? Our attempts to integrate sex
into the rest of our service of God within married life, to
assimilate it into a proper and orderly relation to marriage
within the life of society, have not been so successful that
we can afford to regard ourselves as superior to the generation
which confronted Jesus during His life on earth. Too often in
these matters we have manifested, not a healthy reserve but a
bad conscience. We have tended to be more afraid of the
possible tragedies that could result from the perversion and
abuse of sex, than grateful for the natural possibilities it could
offer to men and women as a gift rightly used and interpreted.
Therefore we have not been able to face the practical problems
of its place and use in life with sufficient frankness, and we have

failed to pass on to the rising generation a balanced and healthy view that they can recognise as worthy of their respect. That our uneasiness is due to an unhealthy suppression of matters that tend to hurt our conscience, rather than to the reserve of faith, is demonstrated by the ease with which it is cashed in upon by the cheap stage comedian, who will revel in a response of nervous giggles about this subject when he is unable to make intelligent jokes about any subject. That such a response is often uncritically given even by those who undoubtedly belong to the most respectable section of our population, seems to be a clear sign that not only the comedian, but the otherwise reputable, belong to an adulterous generation.

But now, in reaction, in the name of a "healthier attitude," we are becoming starkly familiar with the aspects of the problems of sex as they confronted the Apostle Paul in the pagan world surrounding his early churches. We have thrown off not only the artificial restraints created by our bad conscience but also the possibility of any kind of healthy reserve. To such an extent have we divorced it from the service of unselfish love, and harnessed it to self-seeking, that we cannot distinguish between eroticism and love. We have taken it out of what, after all, should be its modest place in the midst of our human life and problems, isolated it, magnified it, made it into the centre of a cult designed to compensate for the drabness of a great deal of the rest of life, and made its most lurid aspects a substitute for culture. We have set sex experience before men and women as something to be sought for its own sake, worked at for what it can give in itself cultivated as an art, or as having a hidden, mystical, "sacramental" value even in the details of its processes. So important has success in such a search become that the possibility of its attainment, or the failure to attain it, has tended to be the criterion of what is good or bad in this sphere.

It is difficult to regard the new development as a good substitute even for the old uneasiness. Certainly it is good to be able to face and discuss as frankly and naturally as possible, the place that sex should have in human life. But there is every sign that this new movement will lead to a lessened ability to sustain lasting and stable married life, and to an increasing difficulty in seeing the relevance of what Jesus Christ came to reveal and offer within the sphere of marriage.

It must be admitted, however, that our traditions in the general relations between men and women have not been good either within the Church, or in the sphere of education, or indeed, in public life generally. There are few pursuits within our social life in which God intended that men should be segregated from women, or women from men. And there are a multitude of the problems of life that rise and could be faced only by people of both sexes together in true fellowship and common action.

But too often has male man hidden himself from the partner whom God placed opposite him, in whose presence alone he can really be himself, with whom he must come to terms if he is to be natural, and with whom he must think and act, if he is to face the problems of life successfully. Too often has male man tried to manage his human affairs without this woman at his side, often in a deliberate flight from her presence. Too often has woman, in reaction, sitting meekly where man has placed her, found in forms often undesirable an effective way of answering the male attempt to dominate. Too often, in further reaction, has the woman tried to be the man, to assert legally her "rights," in ways that seem to imply her own flight from womanhood, and her own refusal to be natural. And it must be admitted that it is still within the sphere of the Church that man can hide most successfully from woman, and woman from man.

2. A new pattern and new possibilities

The Commandment here reminds us, as it must have reminded the people of Israel, that God wants to lay His hand firmly upon all those particular aspects of our social and individual lives that involve the relationships of men and women within and without marriage. He is prepared to help us in this sphere of our life. He wants to put whatever has become disordered here into its true place, and to sanctify the whole for His service.

This is good news indeed. Here at the very point where we

are often very sensitive to destructive and alien influences, where we are reminded very quickly of our failure, where our life is inclined to become easily and radically distorted by self-centredness, God's grace is prepared to meet our human need.

We have already seen how the promise contained in this Commandment has been fulfilled in Jesus Christ. In Him the Word has become "flesh" (Jn. 1.14). This means that God has invaded this realm of flesh and blood which indeed is also the realm of our sex-failure and sex-chaos. God has taken it upon Himself to sanctify our human nature in this very sphere where our human frailty manifests itself so often in fearful distortion and failure. Here where we are primarily "subject to vanity" (Eccl. 1; Rom. VIII.20), we are also subject to the resurrection power of the exalted Jesus Christ who has poured out His Spirit upon all flesh. Here, because God has sent His own son in the likeness of sinful flesh, we can be enabled to walk "not after the flesh but after the Spirit" (Rom. VIII.4–5). "The law of the Spirit of life in Christ Jesus hath made me free from the law of sin and death" (Rom. VIII.2).

What Jesus Christ brings to us and holds out before us as He confronts us with such creative power in and about this particular aspect of our life in this realm of the flesh, is not, however, a new law, but primarily a new pattern. We have discussed in a previous study the main features of this pattern, but it is useful to summarise it again at this point.

For marriage, husband and wife must freely choose each other under the providence of God. Under solemnly covenanted vows they enter into a union of which our best pattern is the close and indissoluble union between Christ and His Church. This union is brought about not simply by the public covenant, or by the self-giving of the two parties one to another within their common life, but also by a creative act of God who really joins them together in such a vital and life-giving unity. To enter and maintain this union in health and richness involves the self-giving of the one to the other in their entire humanity, in soul as well as in body. Of this self-giving the best and truest pattern is the self-giving of Christ to and for His Church. It involves a sharing of hopes and fears, ambitions and service, wealth or poverty. Though this union involves a self-giving within the sex relationship which is natural and good, it also involves equally every other aspect of the human personality. Its stability is based on the faithful forgiving love of each for the other of which the true pattern, again, is found in the love of God for His people and the love of Christ for His Church, and of which the inspiration can only be found in ourselves becoming reconciled to God through Jesus Christ.

This new pattern of marriage casts a wide-spreading light. It illuminates not simply the meaning of marriage in general, but also the meaning of sex and the orientation, communion, and inter-action that the sexes are meant to find as they confront each other within society generally. Moreover, along with such a new pattern of sex relationship, there is given to us, in the presence of Jesus Christ in our midst, a new freedom to conform to this pattern, and to make its fulfilment possible, especially for those who believe in Him.

Because we can thus interpret the commandment as good news, we can now speak confidently to other men about God's will in this sphere of life. In speaking of it we certainly cannot set ourselves up as judges of those who have fallen or are falling. As we speak, we have to remember the warning, "Let him that thinketh he standeth take heed lest he fall" (1 Cor. x.12).

Yet God's call has come to us to witness to what He has done, and can do even here, and we can speak with confidence because within our darkness we have really seen a light, and within our weakness we have really recieved new power and an unfailing promise.

3. The relevance of the pattern for Church, Society, and the individual

The pattern of marriage as we have described it, including the aspects of gift, task, covenant, and fact, has relevance for all marriages within society even for those conducted by civil authorities between men and women who make no profession of the Christian faith. In the sphere of sex and marriage, Jesus Christ has come to heal and restore that which is truly natural. What He gives in this sphere therefore reveals the true meaning of nature as God meant it to be, and made it to be.

Even though men do not believe in Jesus Christ, therefore, they are inevitably blessed by His coming into the midst. They inescapably live in times that He has altered. The sun of Jesus Christ Himself rises upon the evil and the good (Mt. v.45). His healing word can help to meet the concrete needs even of those who have no personal communion with Him (Lk. xvii.11–19). It is surely significant that at Cana of Galilee as He worked in the background of a critical wedding situation, those who benefited most from what he brought to the situation did not seem to be conscious either of His presence or His marvellous work in the midst (Jn. 11.9–10). What is given to a society in the sphere of sex and marriage, even by the Christ who remains very much in the background, perhaps represented by a minority Church which is allowed no more privilege than its mere freedom to exist, is vital and decisive for the welfare of the whole life of that society.

It is therefore to the form of marriage as Christ has revealed it that we must look for the answers to all our marriage problems and for the direction of all our marriage guidance, even when these problems and questions arise from a context that cannot be directly described as Christian. We must seek to understand what marriage is, not by first studying the forms which it takes in different types of society, primitive or civilised, its historical or evolutionary growth, or the codes of law set up for its protection; but by first looking at it in the form in which Jesus Christ sets it before us, and by judging all other forms in this light.

It seems impossible, with the view if marriage that has now emerged, to regard it as a sacrament, a means of communion with Christ to be put on the same level as Preaching, the Lord's Supper, and Baptism. This equation is sometimes made, along with the assertion that since only baptised and professing Christians can enter such a sacramental relationship with one another and with Christ through the Church's ministry, only baptised and professing Christians can be married by the Church. On this view, a civil marriage is regarded as quite a different thing from a Christian marriage.

Certainly all marriages which take place between those who are not Christians are bound to labour under real disadvantages.

They are bound especially to lack the conscious common relationship to God in Christ, and the sense of election to the particular partner and task which are such important aspects of a stable and full marriage union. But even in their imperfect form they often, by the grace of God, have a rich depth which marriages between Christians can sometimes fail to attain.

Certainly, too, the New Testament lays it down that a Christian should not marry an unbeliever. But this is said not because a marriage cannot be achieved between a Christian and an unbeliever, but because there can be no sufficient bond of fellowship or common understanding between such a pair to enable them to proceed on their life's task together without one pulling one way, and the other pulling the other way (II Cor. VI.14–16).

The new pattern given by Jesus Christ for marriage has relevance as we face many of our even more general questions about the relationships between the sexes throughout human society. Here, within marriage in its truest form, we have revealed the primary form of the image of God within human life. But along with this revelation, we have a clear affirmation of fact that must be interpreted generally, that "it is not good that man should be alone" (Gen. II.18). It must now be asserted of male man in general, that he must take account of his "helpmeet" if he is to find the truest part he was meant to play within a social life reflecting God's glory. Even outside marriage, man in general finds himself, as he finds himself oriented and responding to the woman, who is indeed like an indispensable part of himself. She in her turn finds herself as she finds herself made for the man, oriented and responding to him. And the one can no longer be separated from the other (Gen. II.24).

The image of God, in which man was made in the beginning, was an image to be reflected and found primarily in man and woman in their togetherness, and in the mutual response they make the one to the other before God. "So God created man in his own image, in the image of God created he him, male and female created he them" (Gen. I.27). It is freely recognised that, rightly, all do not and cannot (not being called thereto) enter the married state. Their expression of the gift God gave to them in making them either man or woman is therefore given within a much wider context, and within a much more general common activity. In a true general orientation of the sexes one to another, and in each making its truest contribution to the general pattern of society we have another aspect of the true fulfilment of the purpose of the gift of sex.

4. The acceptance of the pattern by Church, Society, and the individual

The Church must gladly acknowledge as true what Jesus Christ brings to light on marriage, and must make the pattern of its conduct in all affairs involving the relationship of the sexes, serve the clear emergence of true Christian marriage as the central feature in its social life. It has no alternative but to reject any teaching or attitude in sex, or any other matter, that would prejudice the clear emergence of such a pattern at the heart of its fellowship. Yet the members of the Church belong at the same time to an "adulterous generation" which still, when it faces and listens to Jesus Christ, wants to protest about the impossibility of acting in accordance with what He sets forth as reality. There can be no ideal solution. We are faced therefore with many problems. We are faced, on the one hand, with the clear pattern of what was "in the beginning" and is meant to be, now and always, in the sphere of marriage— a pattern in which there is no room for divorce. We are faced, on the other hand, with the fact that men and women have become involved in marriages which, either through ignorance, or incompatibility, or sheer unfaithfulness, or sadistic cruelty have been disrupted to such an extent that there is no practical possibility within the realm of common sense of their continuing the task together. We are faced with situations in which one individual seems to be united in fact to two of the opposite sex, and where the most obvious and urgent duty seems to be the severance of the most legitimate liaison in order to leave freedom for the pursuit of the other. We are faced with situations in which a divorced man finds it better to marry again than to "burn" (1 Cor. vii.9). We, too, are faced by the hardness of men's hearts that moved Moses—and the Lord gave him the sanction he required—to allow divorce.

We, too, must therefore allow divorce. The fact that one version of Jesus' teaching on marriage allows the possibility that unfaithfulness could disrupt even an accomplished marriage union (Mt. xix.9) is at least a sign that He was not rigidly legislating when He set forth the pattern He gave to the Apostles, but was rather proclaiming the nature of His Kingdom in its full and wonderful possibilities.

But we cannot allow divorce without reminding ourselves constantly that Jesus Christ has proclaimed that the era of Moses with his free concession to divorce on account of hardness of heart is now at an end. Now that the Kingdom of God has broken into this present world with power, we cannot go back to the Old Testament days. We must now make men, even while they engage in permitted divorce, live in the same tension as made the disciples almost complain to Jesus about the apparent harshness and severity of His words (Mt. xix.10–12). Our greatest sin as a Church in this matter would be so to obscure this clear teaching of Our Lord, and along with it the challenge of the new age of Christ's Kingdom in which we are now living, that divorce and re-marriage could become a comfortable and accepted practice within our Church life. The greatest injustice the Church can do to the teaching of Jesus is to legislate for divorce to take place within its discipline, and thus hinder the clear emergence of the pattern of marriage given by Jesus Christ to be one of the central facts in the life of His Church. The Church must leave itself completely free to witness clearly to the teaching of Jesus Christ in all its aspects.

But the membership of the Church consists of men and women who still, in many aspects of their existence, belong to an adulterous generation. Divorce and remarriage can become a necessity which the Church has to acknowledge, in repentance, even for its own members. The forgiving, healing, mercy of God is so much at work in the present evil world that in many cases the Church will find itself bound to acknowledge a re-marriage after divorce as a true marriage. A divorce, by the grace of God, seems to have happened, and a new union, by the grace of God, seems to have taken place. We can only thank God for this grace given to sinful men like ourselves. But we dare not presume upon acts of the grace of God, or legislate for them to take place. The Church is in a position only to marry, and to acknowledge where a marriage has taken place. The words of our Lord "What therefore God hath joined together, let not man put asunder" (Mt. xix.6) are bound to make it both unwilling to take any action to encourage legal divorce in particular cases, while ready to acknowledge the possibilities that God Himself in His grace can "put asunder".

In adapting its life towards the clear emergence (in its midst) of a true pattern of marriage, the Church is bound to seek from its members in all matters of sex behaviour generally, a pattern of conduct that conforms to this central fact. Marriage cannot be preserved in its healthiest state by a community which allows it to be surrounded by all kinds of sex experimentation or exploration.

It is for this reason that the behaviour required of a Christian in the realm of sex should, at whatever stage of relationship with the other sex, be marked by discipline and self-denial, and should have nothing in it to prejudice the finding of its truest expression within a marriage relationship before God.

It is not difficult to see why the New Testament has no hesitation in asserting that indulgence in fornication within a community is destructive of true marriage within the life of the community, and why it seems to include pre-marital sex intercourse even between engaged couples under this term. In the practice of fornication, sex is inevitably divorced from its true setting in the service of love, and of total personal union, and is linked up with an ultimately fatal self-centredness. This is bound to destroy the mutual respect and honour which, in a very subtle way, must subsist between two persons representing two sexes in marriage from its start. It is bound to destroy the possibility of any true analogy between human marriage and Christ's relationship to His Church, for in His love and self-giving to His people there is no suggestion of any disfiguring vacillation, experimentation, or self-indulgence.

One of the basic reasons for this attitude on the part of the New Testament, however, is the fact of the union of Christ with His members, and their union one with another. In the New Testament, Christians within the Church are regarded as being closely and personally united to Christ, in such a way that Christ dwells in them and they dwell in Christ, being made members of His body. The Lord's Supper and Baptism are visible signs showing the nature of this union, and, indeed, helping to effect it and maintain it. It is in the light of this fact that Paul, for instance, constantly reminds Christians that they are members of Christ and pleads with them not to yield their bodies "as instruments of unrighteousness to sin" but to yield them as "instruments of righteousness unto God" (Rom. vi.13).

The Church is therefore bound to be deeply concerned and quickly sensitive about the conduct of its members in the realm of sex. In the New Testament we are taught that such a thing as an isolated, passing, sex-union between any man and any woman is impossible. Sex relationships always tend to bind people one to another in their totality, and they are creatively designed and ordained by God to do so. Therefore in the abuse of sex, it is possible to deny, weaken or even to cancel, what God is seeking to do through the gift of faith, Baptism, and the Lord's Supper in uniting the members of the Church to Christ and to one another. "Know ye not that your bodies are the members of Christ? shall I then take the members of Christ and make them the members of an harlot? God forbid. What? Know ye not that he which is joined to an harlot is one body? For two, saith he, shall be one flesh" (1 Cor. vi.18–16).

It must now be asked how far anything the Church says to itself or to its own members about marriage and about conduct in sex relationship, can apply to those who are outside the church. How far must the State and secular society conform in its code and attitude, to the patterns revealed in Christ, and manifested and reflected, though often in a very imperfect way, in the life and teaching of the Church? Here the situation is analogous to that which holds with respect to the Sabbath day. The State has to make a decision as to whether the Church, in keeping what it has received from Christ, has or has not entrusted to it something that is of vital importance, not simply for itself, but for all men—even for those who do not as yet believe.

The State, therefore, must decide how far the ideal of marriage within its community life is to conform to that upheld by the Church, and what actual standards in sex behaviour and restraints in the sphere of sex are necessary to stabilise and make possible such a form of marriage. The State can recognise that to encourage a Christian outlook on marriage is for its own good. It can therefore allow the Church complete freedom in its midst, encourage it to propagate the Christian truths about marriage and sex, encourage it to set up at the heart of its community life the Christian home as a light for all men, and to train its children in an outlook on sex and a code of sex behaviour oriented completely to this light, not putting any stumbling block in the way of such training and indeed giving the Church every protection as it seeks to give such training. In this case the ideal of marriage, even amongst those who do not believe, will approximate to the Christian. General sex-behaviour will also tend to contribute towards such an ideal, and law will tend to protect it from deformity. But the State might make a different decision—and there are indications today of a tendency in this direction. The State might decide, for example, to make divorce so easy that the view of marriage as a life partnership would become obscure. It might permit general sex-education of such a nature that sex-experience isolated from marriage would be held out as a healthy ideal of manhood or womanhood, and sex intercourse by couples intending marriage would be encouraged. In such a case the whole general conception of what marriage is within secular society would be lowered, and a real rift would have to be acknowledged between Church and State, as appearing at this point. For the State to make such a decision is a very serious matter. It might indicate that it did not will to give Jesus Christ Himself the freedom, through His Church, to be a living and healing influence in its midst.

Yet the Church cannot expect too much of the State. It cannot expect, for instance, that a State should not take full account of the "hardness of men's hearts" in its divorce laws. The Church indeed, through its pastoral touch with the people, may be able to advise the State where and how relaxation or alteration of the laws are necessary for the sake of justice and humanity. But it must always keep in mind that it cannot hold on to any close relationship with a State which rejects the possibility of receiving healing from it in the sphere of marriage and sex, or which gives itself over to the outlook which characterised gentile paganism in New Testament times.

Any rejection of the Christian pattern by society is a very serious matter. It is sometimes pointed out that when sex is uncontrolled its destructive power is "comparable only with its constructive power when rightly used." Perhaps one of the most important issues on which society has to make a decision in the sphere of sex, on which the Church can give it help, is the extent to which it wills to protect the sense of shame which is instinctively implanted by God as a safeguard against man destroying himself in naturalism (cp Gen. II.25, III.7–11). Bonhoeffer is right in calling this sense of shame, "the underlying fact of sexual life, which, as a natural mode of defence, marks the limit beyond which no alien interference may pass." In this sense of shame, he writes, "expression is given to the essential freedom of the human body in its sexual aspect." The destruction of the sense of shame means the "dissolution of all sexual and conjugal order, indeed of all social order in the widest sense" (*Ethics*, p. 138).

THE EIGHTH COMMANDMENT

Exodus xx.15. *Thou shalt not steal.*

Chapter XII

THE FREEDOM TO SHARE

1. The claim

As we have gone through the Commandments we have found ourselves confronted by a series of divine claims, each upon a different aspect of the common life of the people of God. He has claimed their obedience, service, and witness in the midst of family life, and also through the intimate relationships of sex and marriage. Now He seeks the same service, obedience, and witness in and through their economic life. He lays His hand upon the processes by which their property is acquired and distributed, by which their trade and commerce are carried on, and He says, "Here, too, there must be a response to my goodness and love!"

2. The importance of the claim

The fact that this claim is made, reminds us of the important part played by money and possessions in the life of a man. Man's welfare depends more upon his economic circumstances than those who are comfortably situated sometimes care to admit. There are those who can afford to be "spiritual," and to utter pious warnings against "materialism," only because they themselves are spared the poverty, hunger, and anxiety under which far too many are forced to spend their existence. When God put Adam in the garden of Eden to live a good life, taking care of his welfare, He gave him the free lease of a large property. A human being today needs food, clothing, and a certain amount of leisure from toil, if he is to be able to respond to God in the full way that should characterise his humanity. When Mary Slessor, the missionary, went to the tribes in the interior of Calabar her first desire was to give them food for their souls by preaching the Gospel to them. But she found living conditions such that the moral and spiritual standard of the people facing her could not be raised till their standard of living was raised. She found herself trying to teach them the self-respect that comes from owning property and trading. She showed them her own possessions, her household goods and furniture. She put her clock and sewing machine on exhibition, and it was by inciting the people with a desire to possess property of their own, and to gain a better living by honest trade, that the evangelisation of the province began.

The Bible frankly recognises that money is not enough. "Man doth not live by bread alone, but by every word that proceedeth out of the mouth of the Lord" (Deut. VIII.3; Mt. IV.4). Jesus, both in His teaching and in His active ministry, seemed to give priority to the needs of the soul over the needs of the body. He poured scorn on those who thought that life consisted in the abundance of the things which a man possessed (Lk. XII.15) and therefore neglected the personal relationships which are a far larger part of life. But man does live by bread. In Jesus' own parables we have deeply sympathetic pictures of the tragic plight that men can fall into when they are denied the things that matter for their bodily and social welfare, that of Lazarus lying in misery at the gate of the rich man, and that of the poor defenceless debtor being cast into prison by his merciless creditor, and the wretched unemployed, hanging about the market place idle because no man had hired them (Lk. XVI.19–31, VII.36–50; Mt. XX.1–16). The prayer He taught His disciples has the clause, "give us each day our daily bread," even before that about the forgiveness of sins (Mt. VI.11–12).

3. The background against which the claim is made

The background against which this claim of God, "Thou shalt not steal," was constantly made throughout the life of Israel, was one in which there always tended to appear extreme differences in wealth and poverty. Throughout the history of Israel it was far too often the rule, which made its exceptions all the more striking, that those who had position, ability and resources, instead of using them for the good of their neighbours, were tempted to use them to draw into their own power and possession what their brother possessed too. As a result of this, the poorer member of the community, made economically weak either through folly, misfortune, or inheritance could not resist the sheer pressure of the economic processes, and became more and more dispossessed of property, of free access to the common resources of the community, and finally of all liberty and power to live a full and good life.

Jesus, in his parable, described Dives, the rich man, faring so sumptuously every day that the crumbs which fell from his table would have been a feast for a normal person, and Lazarus lying at his gate neglected by all but the dogs, forced to live by begging from those who might have pity on him when they saw the open sores on his body (Lk. xvi.19–23). In giving us this picture, He was describing what had been a permanent feature of life within Israel as it developed throughout the centuries. Even Israel's early laws had to take account of some men becoming so destitute and desperate, that they sold their own daughters into slavery, and finally plunged their whole family into ruin (Ex. xxi. 7; ii Kings iv. 1). As the wealth of the country developed through trade and commerce, instead of benefiting all members of the community, it tended to flow into the hands of those at the top of the social scale, where it largely remained. Solomon set up a splendid court, and launched an impressive programme of public building and developing administration, but a large proportion of the money he needed to see his plan through had to come from people who derived no real benefit from it. In the book of Amos, we have a picture of the northern Kingdom a generation or two later. In it we see the rich, now possessing summer houses and winter houses, stretched out in idleness on their beds of ivory, with the wine flowing and the hired musicians playing at their pleasure, while they eat the lambs from the flock and the calves from the stalls. But all the while in the background, agents are at work in a dreadful policy of oppressing the poor who have already been bled to produce the wealth that is now directed against them. They buy the poor for silver and the needy for a pair of shoes, and sell the refuse of the wheat, and lie down on the pledges (Am. ii.8; iii.15, iv.1, v.11, viii.4). Not long after this, in the southern Kingdom, Isaiah has to pronounce woes on the rich "that join house to house, that lay field to field, till there be no room, and ye be made to dwell alone in the midst of the land," that is, till those who have been bought out of their homesteads are driven either into exile or forced into economic slavery under those who "grind the face of the poor" (cp. Is. 1.17, III.15, v.8). Later on, in the time of Nehemiah, we find those who possessed wealth exacting usury of their poorer brethren in defiance of the Law of God, and the poor borrowing money to meet their taxes, mortgaging their fields and vineyards, and falling into the hands of other men, as their families went into serfdom.

On a world scale, the same Dives–Lazarus state of affairs prevailed within international relations. It did not take long for Egypt, the wealthy nation, its granaries stocked with food and sharing its plenty with the surrounding peoples, to change into the harsh aggressive imperial power, bent on its own aggrandisement, enslaving the people it had formerly protected and attracted to its borders, and becoming wealthier by the tribute it could exact and the labour it could force out of those whom it had made its slaves (cp. Gen. XLV.16–20; Ex. 1.8–14).

Some would say that this state of affairs within Israel's life was simply the inevitable historical accompaniment of its gradual development from a simple nomadic or agrarian society into a community organised and settled around a city. But there are some very obvious social and psychological reasons for asserting that in this state of affairs we have a picture of an unhealthy feature that will tend to make its appearance in every kind of human society at any stage in its development. There is always within society, an unequal distribution of human ability. A man like Jacob, for instance, will always be able, through his superior skill, craft and brilliance not only to create new wealth around him, but to draw to himself what belongs to Esau and even to Laban. There will always be many who have little initiative and drive, and some who are indeed incapable of keeping even what others put, in charity, into their hands.

Moreover, within the human heart there is a deep sense of insecurity, a basic anxiety. It appears chiefly in the rich.

Indeed, the wealthier and more powerful a man becomes, the more he has to be anxious over, and the more acute his anxiety becomes. Therefore he always wants to secure himself more and more through possessing more and more (cp. Lk. xii.17–19). The more he has, often the more his tastes develop, as he discovers the variety of uses to which he can put his wealth, therefore what satisfied him at one stage in his life is now neither big enough nor distinct enough, to satisfy him as his wealth increases. That such was the case in Israel is seen from the Prophets' descriptions, often bitterly sarcastic of the rich in Israel, their life and ways, their clothes, personal ornaments, and entourage, their "haughtiness," their desire to glory over others through sheer possession (cp. Is. iii.16 ff., xxii.18).

Perhaps some features of this economic state of affairs are due to a property in money itself. It has been pointed out that though water left to itself always tends to flow downwards, money, on the contrary always tends to flow upwards to those who have it. The more therefore that a man possesses of it and the more of it he can control, the more power he has to draw to himself the wealth of other people and to control their economic life, and the more he seems to want to do so. The cause of this phenomenon and the extent to which it is a good thing or a bad thing has been disputed, and will be disputed, as long as the science of economics and the practice of politics last. But undoubtedly in the long run it tends to create the undesirable background of extreme differences between wealth and poverty against which the claim of this Commandment had to be reasserted time and again in the history of Israel.

4. The witness of the true Israel

That such things should happen in the life of Israel was in contradiction to everything that God had meant when He redeemed them and made them His people. Prophet after Prophet reminded them of this. They were a nation called to give a better witness to the love of God for all men, and especially for the poor, than any other nation on earth. It was not the true Israel but a false Israel that allowed such oppressive things to happen in their economic life.

This Eighth Commandment is bound to be interpreted in this context. It is primarily directed against the robbery of the poor by the rich. For us "stealing" most often means the robbery of the rich by the poor, and the word tends to denote the activity of the highwayman, the burglar, the embezzler, and the petty thief. But in fact, though such ways are never condoned, only a few times are woes uttered in the Bible against them, while in page after page judgment is called down on those who "take away the right from the poor of the people, who prey upon the widows and rob the fatherless" (Is. x.2).

It could be argued that, according to the Bible, to refuse to make a due contribution to the needy is to steal. We have a hint of this in Paul's application of this Commandment to the Ephesians "Let him that stole, steal no more; but rather let him labour, working with his hands the things which is good, that he may have to give to him that needeth" (Eph. IV.28). "The needy shall not always be forgotten. The expectation of the poor shall not perish for ever" (Ps. IX.18). "Thou shalt neither vex a stranger nor oppress him: for ye were strangers in the land of Egypt. Ye shall not afflict any widow or fatherless child. If thou afflict them in any wise and they cry unto me, I will surely hear their cry; and my wrath shall wax hot, and I will kill you with the sword; and your wives shall be widows and your children fatherless. If thou lend money to any of my people that is poor by thee, thou shalt not be to him as an usurer neither shalt thou lay upon him usury. If thou at all take thy neighbour's raiment to pledge, thou shalt deliver it unto him by that the sun goeth down" (Ex. XXII.21–6).

It is in and through such verses as these, that we begin to understand the primary meaning of the Commandment. It is addressed to men who have all equally shared in the redeeming love and purpose of God. "I have not redeemed your brother in order that he might lie starving and exposed under your feet. Nor have I been specially generous to you, in order to put power in your hands further to afflict him. Give to your brother what he needs for his welfare out of what you have, for what you have is mine, and to withhold your hand from him is to steal from me!" "The poor," says a great Old Testament scholar in a comment on this, "are to receive their rights, not as a form of charitable largesse, but as a fundamental means of preserving national life and the most important provision for its safety. It is more important than large battalions and powerful allies, that the nation should allow its weak and helpless members to share in the freedom and justice given them by the mighty hand of God" (Eichrodt, *Biblical Interpretation Today*, pp. 262–3).

Several features of the legislation in Israel stand out in contrast to much of our present day practice. One is the fact that legislation was used not only to prevent irresponsible sources of power from exploiting the labour and weakness of others, but also in a deliberate attempt to prevent the occurrence of extreme differences in wealth and poverty.

The land, access to which offered the basic source of the ordinary man's livelihood, was regarded as belonging to God, and as lent by God to the people. "The land shall not be sold for ever; for the land is mine; for ye are strangers and sojourners with me" (Lev. xxv.23). It was therefore meant to be divided up for the benefit of all, so that every man could share in the opportunities of livelihood and employment within the community. This basic principle was safeguarded by laws forbidding the permanent sale of his property by a man in debt. The debtor's land could be taken from him for some years, but every seventh year all debts were to be released and men returned to their land (Deut. xv.1–3; Lev. xxv.10, 28). In order to prevent the accumulation of debt by one man to another usury was forbidden (Ex. xxii.25–7; Deut. xxiii.20). It was admitted that there would be men who would lose their land through folly or sheer inability, and who themselves also might be sold into slavery. But in this condition, again, six years was the maximum period of compulsory bondage (Ex. xxi.2–6; Deut. xv.12–18), and in the seventh year the man was offered his freedom. Constantly the law sought to redress the situation in which men, through either folly or misfortune on the one hand, or through greed or good fortune on the other hand, could exploit one another through the manipulation of property and possessions. It was recognised that there must come a stage in social affairs when consideration of the sanctity of a man's person should overrule consideration of the sanctity of acquired property.

5. The new order within the old

The world of today is in many respects little different from
that against which the economic witness of Israel was meant
to be given. We have in play today the same acquisitive
tendencies spurred on by the same basic sense of instability,
and the same tendency to glory in mere possession. This leads
to the same struggle for existence in which wealth seems to be
able to attract more wealth, and the astute seem to have
remarkable ability to succeed in the struggle. Those of us who
have experience of pastoral work will know how easily wealth,
in its flow upwards, tends to leave the economically defenceless
in a poor plight indeed.

It is obvious that in our modern economic structures we
cannot go back to the ideal pattern of Israel's life. We would
have no grounds for imposing on our present system the aboli-
tion of interest on loans, and the cancellation of all debts every
fifty years. How far then is it possible in the midst of modern
society to bring to bear the economic challenge we find in the
Bible? We can certainly call for a constant watchfulness by
government over the direction and strength of the flow of
wealth, so that it will turn downwards as much as upwards,
and while it is easy to preach a short-cut to Utopia through
some-one else's property, we can nevertheless proclaim that the
right of every man to a measure of economic freedom, to access
to the means by which he can live, is more fundamental than
the right of every man to the liberty to draw the wealth of
others to himself.

But there are indications that even more can be expected of
Christians. A sign was given just after the day of Pentecost,
that the presence of the kingdom of God in the midst of this
world's life, could produce precisely the economic witness that
this world needs. We read that after the Spirit had been poured
out upon the Christians, "all that believed were together, and
had all things common; and sold their possessions and goods,
and parted them to all men, as every man had need" (Acts
II.44–5). This is not the attempt to set up an early Christian
communistic community. There is no compulsive law, or
theory, behind the sharing of possessions and wealth that took

place here. It is an affair of the heart. The acquisitive tendency has been strangely, suddenly and decisively reversed, and this has produced dramatic effects in the economic behaviour of men.

Besides the powerful working of the Spirit in the hearts of the disciples there was also the example of Christ. His whole redeeming work was an act of sheer generous outpouring to others of everything He possessed. Therefore in the early Church no one could be His disciple with any sincerity or comfort, and not somehow become ashamed of the covetousness that draws what should be for others into the centre of the self. They felt themselves bound, as His disciples, to reproduce the pattern of His out-flowing generosity in a new open-handedness. "See that ye abound in this grace also," wrote Paul to the Corinthians in an attempt to encourage them in this new kind of liberality in giving, "For ye know the grace of the Lord Jesus Christ, that, though he was rich, yet for your sakes he became poor, that ye through his poverty might be rich" (II Cor. VIII.7-9). Here is surely the beginning of a solution to the economic problems of our own day,—the beginning of the transformation of the dictatorship of wealth into the stewardship of wealth.

If we are to begin to live in the power and light of this new order of things, we must constantly remember the promise in the face of which this Commandment is given. If God has indeed set His love upon us and redeemed us, then He will provide for us. Our earthly needs are covered by a providence that will never fail even in the direst of straits. Therefore we do not need to steal, with the tactics of either the pickpocket or the pilferer, the burglar, the embezzler, the street bandit, or the falsefier of income tax returns. We do not need to go on and on, pulling the wealth of the community in towards ourselves without at the same time, and with an even flow, letting it move out again to serve the community to which it belongs more than to ourselves. We do not need to try to steal from God by retaining for our own selfish use a far too large proportion of the wealth He has given us for the service of our fellow men.

THE NINTH COMMANDMENT

EXODUS xx.16. *Thou shalt not bear false witness against thy neighbour.*

reputation, personal character – (case of CIA,

White House keeping truth for people – sometime necessary, but not to substitute for it a lie.

USSR –

Chapter XIII

THE FREEDOM OF THE TRUTH

1. The power of the lie

IN the book of Isaiah, the prophet indulges in biting sarcasm about the politicians of his day who constantly used lies to conceal the compromise and contradictions in their policies, and to shelter themselves from blame, and who were so alarmingly successful in doing this, that they thought themselves secure for ever. "We have made a covenant with death, and with hell are we at agreement; when the overflowing scourge shall pass through, it shall not come unto us: for we have made lies our refuge, and under falsehood have we hid ourselves" (Is. xxviii.15).

Lord Coleraine, discussing the present situation in international politics, speaks of "the power of the lie in the modern world." "The lie has commonly been accepted as a political instrument," he writes; "there is nothing new in that. What is new, is that in our day it is so thinly disguised and so widely believed" (quoted from Herklots: *The Ten Commandments*, p. 149). We need to live abroad only for a short time to discover how deeply imbedded in our own minds, through wrong and inadequate reports, are false conceptions of life in the other country, and how deeply imbedded in the minds of other people through false and inadequate reports, are entirely wrong ideas of the life and attitude of the British.

The reasons for this are various. When the malicious and prejudiced have power, they can use our mass means of communication, the press, the radio, and television to spread distortion of the truth on a colossally planned scale. Moreover, there is a weakness in human nature, and a defect in the public mind, which far too readily consents and surrenders to such abuse. Many men in their hearts do not care enough for the truth to fight passionately for it when they know it is being distorted, finally they begin to accept, and even to enjoy, the lie. The public mind can easily become conditioned to respond uncritically to blaring party headlines, and catchy advertising slogans, without regard for truth. Under such circumstance it is not surprising that the means of propaganda within a country so often become controlled by those who have no other concern than to sell goods by fair means or foul, or by those with powerful vested interests in political or commercial dictatorship. Subjected to their methods and propaganda, the public mind acquires a taste for what is given to it. It responds more and more with its custom and support where there is an exaggerated emphasis on the sexy or the sadistic or otherwise sordid. It would rather have the juice of sensationalism than the bones of truth. And so the conditions for a final distortion of the truth are ripe, the beast can rise out of the abyss, and people not only forget that ever there was a Ninth Commandment, but cease to realise that one was ever needed.

The main reason why the lie sticks so powerfully, is the basic fact that in this world, as we have made it, there is a darkness that hates the light and that seeks constantly to master and extinguish the light (Jn. 1.5). Do we not each of us at times find that this spirit of darkness is part of ourselves, and has a breeding place in our own minds and hearts, making us want to "call evil good, and good evil" (Is. v.20)? Our minds are prone to feed upon false prejudices, and to dislike the truth which too often judges us and proves us wrong. Therefore, like many in the Gospel stories, we want to oppose the truth as it shines in Jesus. If "the lie sticks," it finds a convenient and easy sticking place within the human mind. If truth is to flourish, and have free currency, it can flourish only in a conflict against darkness.

2. The things that are at stake when truth is at stake

A judicial tribunal in Britain recently called witnesses, in order to find out the truth in a matter about which the Press had published most alarming and damaging reports, reflecting on the good name of more than one Minister of the Crown. In the course of the proceedings, two journalists refused to disclose the source from which they had received certain information

Surely, we can argue that ...

which they had passed on to newspapers, and which had been given circulation. Their plea was that to name the source of their information would be breaking confidence with friends who had trusted them to keep their identity secret. The journalists were sent to prison for their refusal to tell the tribunal the information they required if they were to pursue their inquiries and find out the whole truth. There has been, since then, a good deal of discussion as to whether they should have been treated in this way, and many vigorous protests have been made about their sentence. But we can argue that even loyalty to a friend cannot outweigh the vital importance of a clear and extremely urgent public duty. Surely men who love truth will be deeply concerned that truth should be given a chance to be established at a time when truth is very much at stake in public life, in press circles, and in politics. There are times when for the sake of the health of society, it becomes important to uncover every possible source of lying and wild rumour. So damaging can be the encouragement of the lie, that it would be tragic indeed if the law of the land gave special protection to that which fears the light. Under the present circumstances it seems justifiable to risk a lesser injustice in attempting to redress an exceedingly grave one.

When truth is at stake in public life, much more than the truth is in danger. This was realised even in Old Testament times, and it gave their laws on this matter a severe and unrelenting note that sometimes shocks modern readers. "If an unrighteous witness rise up against a man to testify against him of wrong doing, then both the men between whom the controversy is, shall stand before the Lord, before the priests and judges which shall be in those days, and the judges shall make diligent inquisition. And behold if the witness be a false witness, and hath testified falsely against his brother then shall do to him as he had thought to do to his brother, and thou shalt put away the evil from the midst of thee, and those that remain shall hear and fear and shall henceforth commit no such evil in the midst of thee, and thine eye shall not pity. Life shall go for life, eye for eye, tooth for tooth, hand for hand, foot for foot" (Deut. xix.16–21). As far as the furtherance of, and entrance into, the Kingdom of God is concerned, the "eye for an eye . . ." must now be radically qualified, especially when it is a matter of a Christian's own personal attitude to any who have wronged him (Mt. v.38–48). But there can be no qualification of the "diligent inquisition" needed by fair lawcourts, and of the need of men to "hear and fear," when society is faced with a threat to the free currency of truth in its midst. A Cabinet Minister speaking in the midst of a further recent political crisis which raised doubts in the public mind about the truth of solemn affirmations made by responsible ministers in Parliament, attributed the success of the political system of Britain to the "solid tradition of honest dealing and truthful speaking" which is "the foundation of Parliamentary life." "Free institutions . . .," he said, "dissolve into violence and chaos except upon a basis of mutual trust" (Lord Hailsham, as he then was, reported in the *Scotsman*, 15 June 1963).

But freedom is not the only casualty when truth is at stake. Under circumstances that breed the cynical assumption that all men are liars, it must be doubted whether any good and spontaneous culture can flourish, or whether any of the good and beautiful things of human life that depend on a healthy and stable intercourse between men can be given currency. In this matter, the interaction between the Press and public opinion is as important as what goes on in Parliament. If truth is to be served, the Press must report matters with conscientious accuracy, avoid giving mere rumour the semblance of truth, and give due emphasis to matters that are of real importance. Public opinion must be trained to react with a determined "consumer resistance" against the petty peddling in newsprint of lies and of the mere gossip that has no other value than its salaciousness.

When truth is at stake, something of very great value to the individual is also at stake. God desires every man to have honour and a good name amongst his fellows, just as He desires for Himself honour and a name amongst the creatures He has made. In the Third Commandment He seeks to protect His own name from dishonour. In this Ninth Commandment He seeks likewise to protect the good name of every man who wills to receive such a gift.

Who steals my purse steals trash . . .
But he that filches from me my good name
Robs me of that which not enriches him
And makes me poor indeed.

Good men will not spontaneously give their friendship and
confidence to a man who has no good name. Nor will they
trust his word or put themselves under his influence. The man
who has lost his name has therefore lost something vital to him
as a social being. He is condemned to a life of isolation in the
midst of the society whose life he knows he was made to share.

   In the Bible, more than anywhere else, the importance is
understood of every man's having a name held in honour and
esteem among his fellows. "A good name rather is to be chosen
than great riches, and loving favour rather than silver and
gold" (Prov. xxii.1). "A good name is better than precious
ointment" (Eccl. vii.1). Even Saul, after he had been rejected
by God and had lost his Kingdom, clung on to Samuel in
a last desperate effort to save at least some semblance of a
good name amongst his people, and cried "Honour me now,
I pray thee, before the elders of my people and before Israel"
(1 Sam. xv.30). The psalmists, time and again, appear to suffer
more from evil rumours about themselves, than from any other
affliction. Even in the New Testament, we have Paul always
careful to vindicate his reputation against the slanders that
were spreading about him. A very large element in the suffering
of Christ arose from His suffering the complete loss of His
name, reputation, and honour. No true human society can be in-
different to this essential element in enabling the individual to
live a full and free human life in its midst. Even for this alone,
it must allow free currency to the truth and abhor the lie.

3. The final eclipse and triumph of truth

   Within this conflict of light against darkness in which the
life of mankind is involved, the truth about Jesus Christ is also
involved. The most apparently successful assault of darkness
against the light was, and is, directed against Him and against
His Gospel. It is deeply significant that, before he handed over

Jesus to the Jewish authorities and the mob to be crucified, Pontius Pilate not only washed his hands, but he also uttered the famous question, "What is truth?" (Jn. xviii.38). It must have been uttered sceptically. Pilate was well acquainted with the cynicism prevailing in the political and ecclesiastical atmosphere in which the events around him were taking place. He knew no one who really cared that truth should be known, that light should triumph over darkness, or that justice should really be done. He could see through the High Priest and his other little priests. He could see through to the motives that had at last made the Pharisees for once agree with the Sadducees and unite with them. He knew what was in this mob from past sad experience. Perhaps he knew that even the disciples of Jesus, even Peter, had shown up badly in the struggle of truth against falsehood. "What is truth?"

In such an atmosphere where there are none who really care for truth, Jesus was bound to be rejected. Here the One who is the "Truth" died, His light obscured by darkness, of no reputation, the victim of false witnesses, of the tongues of the slanderers, of a whispering campaign inspired by subtle political propaganda. Even His disciples, overwhelmed for a moment by the general atmosphere, bore false witness. Can we hope for anything better today where truth is not cared for? Today, wherever the darkness that hates the light flourishes, it is bound to find the chief target for its venom in the point where the light shines brightest, and where untruth and darkness are most threatened. Therefore today, the Gospel is still the light which untruth and darkness hate most. The fate of the Gospel in any society is more closely bound up with the fate of human liberty, and with the freedom of truth and culture than we often imagine.

Wherever an attack is made on the free currency of truth in any form or in any sphere of life, it is bound to be very soon directed against the free currency of the truth about Jesus. This is why every form of dictatorship is bound to attack the Gospel, and this is why, in so many spheres of the world's life, Jesus Christ, and the truth about Him, is still the target of men's lies.

In spite of its eclipse even in our modern society, no amount of falsehood can ultimately destroy truth or even alter it in the smallest aspect. It remains the same and is bound ultimately to be revealed (Rom. ii.16). The darkness cannot overmaster the light (Jn. 1.5). Indeed, even within the course of history it is so strong in its ability to witness for itself that even the lies that are told against it ultimately witness for it. God used the falsehood of the High Priest and his witnesses, and of Pilate, to further the Gospel. Even the slanderous and thoughtless gibes of the onlookers bore witness to the glory of Jesus rather than to His shame. "We can do nothing against the truth, but for the truth" (ii Cor. xiii.8). Therefore neither the truth of Christ, nor its ultimate triumph, is at stake when a community rejects the truth. What is at stake, however, where truth has ceased to be cared for, is the healing presence of Jesus Christ in the midst of a community that needs Him more than it can know.

4. Where our repentance must begin

Truth, even when it is being publicly called in question, seeks all the more urgently the witness of the individual. The Commandment challenges us each in a very particular way about how we are dealing in this matter with respect to our "neighbour." Here we must not become lost in generalities. We must begin where we are. When we meet our friends or our social groups in conversation, and a name comes up for discussion, this man concerned is our neighbour. Here our obedience to this command is at stake, and here, if anywhere, the course that truth has to take in maintaining itself, is at stake.

We must remember not only the importance of this man's name for his true well-being, but also the fact that it is we, his neighbours, who make or mar his name. Man was not made to bear witness to himself. Unlike God, man is made to shine not in his own light, but in the light which falls on him from outside, and proceeds from him through his neighbours' witness. God has placed him close to us in life so that we might give him the good name he needs to have. We are the authority which can make or mar his name, his career and his happiness. The nearer we are to him, the more we have access to him, then the greater is the authority of our word about him. His "name" is formed or confirmed by our reports, or by our consenting to other reports, or by our failure to correct false reports. "A lie would soon come to nothing from its own emptiness, and fall to the ground," says Calvin, "if it were not taken up and supported by the unrighteous consent of others."

It is here at this precise point that we often prove ourselves weak and unable to move against the stream. Indeed here to a surprising degree, we Christians prove ourselves no better than the world, in our love for exaggeration, in our desire to be first in with a good story, in our ability to express malice and ill-will with an air of innocent regret. This is why both the Old and the New Testament are surprisingly detailed and completely up to date in their description of our weakness and our behaviour. "Thou shalt not go up and down as a talebearer among thy people: neither shalt thou stand against the blood of thy neighbour: I am the Lord" (Lev. xix.16). "Thou shalt not raise a false report: put not thine hand with the wicked to be an unrighteous witness. Thou shalt not follow a multitude to do evil; neither shalt thou speak in a cause to decline after many to wrest judgment" (Ex. xxiii.1–2). "The words of a talebearer are as wounds, and they go down into the innermost parts of the belly" (Prov. xviii.8). "Even so the tongue is a little member, and boasteth great things. Behold, how great a matter a little fire kindleth! And the tongue is a fire, a world of iniquity; so is the tongue among our members, that it defileth the whole body, and setteth on fire the course of nature; and it is set on fire of hell. For every kind of beasts, and of birds, and of serpents, and of things in the sea, is tamed, and hath been tamed of mankind: But the tongue can no man tame; it is an unruly evil, full of deadly poison. Therewith bless we God, even the Father; and therewith curse we men, which are made after the similitude of God" (Jas. iii.5–9).

It is here, however, at this precise point that we are given wise advice and stern warning. "Meddle not with him that flattereth with his lips" (Prov. xx.19). "Where no wood is the fire goeth out: so where there is no whisperer the strife ceaseth" (Prov. xxvi.20). "A talebearer revealeth secrets, but he that is of a faithful spirit concealeth the matter"

(Prov. xi.13). "I say unto you, that every idle word that men shall speak, they shall give account thereof in the day of judgment. For by thy words thou shalt be justified, and by thy words thou shalt be condemned" (Mt. xii.36–7). "Therefore whatsoever ye have spoken in darkness shall be heard in the light; and that which ye have spoken in the ear in closets shall be proclaimed upon the housetops" (Lk. xii.3). Here at this point, too, we are given an excellent prayer and shown an excellent way, and are given an excellent reason for it. "Set a watch, O Lord, before my mouth: keep the door of my lips (Ps. cxli.3). "Wherefore putting away lying, speak every man truth with his neighbour: for we are members one of another" (Eph. iv.25).

5. The power of true witness in the service of Christ

The challenge to us to speak the truth about our neighbour involves us, in a peculiar way, in bearing true witness to Jesus Christ. God has not only put our neighbour's good name in our hands, He has Himself become our neighbour in Jesus, and has thus put His own good name in our hands.

Jesus Christ is the neighbour to each of us. In becoming a man and a neighbour, He became in a real way dependent on the witness of others. This is why He chose to have around Him on earth, twelve men, into whose hands He put His name. He lived close to them, spoke to them, revealed His heart to them, made them the witnesses of His sufferings and their meaning, of His resurrection and its meaning, and when He was finally leaving them He said, "Ye shall be witnesses unto me" (Acts i.8). They were the men who were to give Him a name in this world. They had His reputation in their hands. What they would report and confirm about Him would determine the name He was to have throughout the ages of earth's history.

When Jesus chose and trained these twelve men, His first concern was simply to choose and train men who would not bear false witness against their neighbour, men of integrity who could make a true judgment about what was happening before their eyes and give a faithful report about what they had seen and heard (1 Jn. i.1). He was not concerned to have about Him men who were naturally clever or good at subtle argument, but simply men whom He could trust not to distort, or exaggerate, or withhold what they had seen and heard. His Gospel does not need to be supported or illuminated by any light other than its own. It requires and seeks and is served best by men who will simply witness to the truth of its own light. It is when we understand the necessity Jesus had of such witness around Him, that we can understand the importance of this Commandment within the life of Israel, as a means of preparation for the people of God.

We must remind ourselves that there is the same call to us, as the people of God today, to give faithful witness to Jesus Christ. If we have confessed His name, and identified ourselves with His Gospel and His Church, we cannot fail to bear a witness of one kind or another. Our words, our conduct and our attitudes are constantly measured against our profession, and an assessment is made of the worth of the name we have confessed. When Jesus was on trial, before His crucifixion, "many bare false witness against him," says Mark (Mk. xiv.56). His own disciples are bound to be included in this deeply suggestive comment, for they failed to stand by Him and speak the truth. Therefore when Jesus was asked by the High Priest to tell him "of his disciples, and of his doctrine," He could attempt to justify Himself only on the question of His teaching and His forced silence about His disciples could not fail to be noted by those who watch for such things (Jn. xviii.19–20).

We must remind ourselves, too, that what is required in a witness is truth and reliability. Sometimes in our attempt to achieve attractiveness and modernity in our witness, we obscure and distort the simple truth. In the giving of witness it would be better to think of ourselves as on oath in a court of law, rather than on trial before an audience where a popularity vote is to be cast. Is a true witness not bound to discard all thought of popularity?

But we must remind ourselves that, in spite of the inevitably false and distorted witness that we give, even with our best efforts, Jesus Christ, through the Spirit, overcomes the compromise and confusion in which we so often find ourselves. While men bore false witness to Him, and thus to themselves as well, He Himself gave a sufficiently true, clear and strong witness before God and man to the real meaning and greatness of the destiny that human life was to find in Himself. Since that witness has been given, everything despairing or contemptuous or cynical in the attitude or witness of man to man can be proved false in the light of it. It is in witnessing to Jesus Christ that henceforth we can bear the only true witness to our fellow men—and this miracle can still indeed take place through us by the grace of God and the power of the Spirit. "When the Comforter is come, whom I will send unto you from the Father, even the Spirit of truth," said Jesus to His disciples, ". . . he shall testify of me: and ye also shall bear witness" (Jn. xv. 26–27). "Ye shall receive power after that the Holy Ghost is come upon you: and ye shall be witnesses unto me both in Jerusalem, and in all Judea, and in Samaria, and unto the uttermost parts of the earth" (Acts 1.8).

THE TENTH COMMANDMENT

EXODUS XX. 17. *Thou shalt not covet thy neighbour's house, thou shalt not covet thy neighbour's wife, nor his manservant, nor his maidservant, nor his ox, nor his ass, nor anything that is thy neighbour's.*

Chapter XIV

THE FREEDOM OF THE HEART

1. The heart of God's demand

A RICH young ruler ran up to Jesus and asked Him "Good master what shall I do to inherit eternal life?" In reply, our Lord quoted the five Commandments which precede this last one. "Thou knowest the commandments," He said, "Do not commit adultery, Do not kill, Do not steal, Do not bear false witness, Honour thy father and thy mother" (Lk. XVIII.20). The young man's reply was without hesitation, and we cannot doubt his sincerity in giving it. "All these," he said, "have I kept from my youth up."

But we must note that Jesus, in His selection from the Commandments, omitted to quote this last one: "Thou shalt not covet." If Jesus had quoted this too, the young man would not have been able to reply so confidently. Indeed it was precisely on the ground of the Tenth Commandment that Jesus proceeded to challenge him in the conversation that followed. He challenged him about his possessions and their hold on his heart. He challenged him to go and sell all he had to prove whether he was not holding on covetously to what should have been given to the poor. He challenged him so pointedly that the young man, no longer able to speak with him, turned away sorrowful.

If we isolate the previous five Commandments—which challenge us about our behaviour to our neighbour—from this Tenth Commandment, we too, may be able to measure our life against them and say, "all these have I kept." But if we listen carefully to this Tenth Commandment, and interpret the other Commandments in the light of this Tenth, then we are all of us confused, and, indeed, lost. For this Commandment challenges us not simply about our outward acts of behaviour but about the desires of our hearts. It challenges us as to what we are thinking, what we are wanting, what we dream about. It challenges us about what wells up from the subconscious, and it says, "God seeks to be Lord within this realm too!"

Here in the Tenth Commandment we come to the heart of what it means to face God's demand upon the whole of our life. Here at the end of the Commandments, we find out where God expects us to begin to serve Him. This is a sensible order. God in the First Commandment makes a total demand upon the heart and soul and strength and life of His people. Then in the next eight Commandments, He defines all the areas of life in which He seeks for them to express this devotion and commitment. Then, in the last Commandment, He makes another total and radical demand, reminding us that if we are going to serve God at all in these areas of life on which He has laid His hand, we must serve Him with the heart as well as with the outward life, we must obey Him in spirit as well as in letter. Therefore, though this Commandment adds nothing new to what has been already implied in all the other Commandments, it brings out everything that is most important in the sight of God, and sends us back again to the other Commandments with a new understanding of their meaning. It keeps us from becoming superficial. It says to us what the prophet once said to Israel, addressing them as a people always tempted to put God off with what was only on the surface, "Rend your heart and not your garments, and turn to the Lord your God" (Joel II.14).

It is from Jesus Himself, that we learn most forcibly how the previous Commandments must be interpreted in the light of the Tenth Commandment. "Ye have heard that it was said by them of old time, Thou shalt not kill; and whosoever shall kill shall be in danger of the judgment: But I say unto you, that whosoever is angry with his brother without a cause shall be in danger of the judgment. . . . Ye have heard that it was said by them of old time, Thou shalt not commit adultery: but I say unto you, that whosoever looketh on a woman to lust after her hath committed adultery with her already in his heart" (Mt. v.21–2, 27–8). It is not enough to refrain outwardly from stealing, killing, and adultery if in our heart we are stealing, killing, and committing adultery.

Here is where God's judgment differs from man's judgment. "Repent therefore of this thy wickedness," said Peter to a man whom he was calling to repentance, "and pray God if perhaps the thought of the heart may be forgiven thee" (Acts VIII.22). Man tends to limit his prayer to "God forgive what I have done and said," but we must pray: "God forgive our hearts for being what they are." Man, in measuring the significance or success of a work, or a life, or a church, is content with what can be seen, tabulated, pointed to, spoken about, or made the data for advertisement. But God measures the motives, the inner sacrifice, the inner cost in suffering and tears.

In taking us in this way to the heart of God's demand upon us, the Tenth Commandment helps us all to discover that we are, and will ever remain while this life lasts, sinners before God. Luther in his catechism pointed out that this was one of the purposes of this Commandment. It is directed not primarily to the openly and avowedly bad people in the world such as robbers, adulterers, and liars, but is directed to the pious who tend to praise themselves that they have kept all the previous Commandments.

2. The heart of the human problem

And so from the heart of God's demand, we are led to the heart of the human problem. Here in this Commandment the Word of God proves itself "quick and powerful, and sharper than any two-edged sword, piercing even to the dividing asunder of soul and spirit," and "a discerner of the thoughts and intents of the heart" (Heb. IV.12). As we bring this word of God to bear on our own hearts, and seek, in the light of it and under its pressure, to reform our hearts and bring them into obedience, we find ourselves not only guilty as to the past but also without any hope for the future. No one can stand before God with his heart open, in the light of this Commandment. It faces us with the fact that there is something incurably perverse within us, something we cannot either of ourselves or with any known natural resources, transform or even bring into good order and decency.

It was when he measured his life against this Commandment

that the Apostle Paul was brought into a state of deep despair. He was like the rich young ruler, only more so. He, above all other men, had made scrupulous, noble, and long-sustained efforts to keep the Ten Commandments so that he might please God and inherit eternal life. In this pursuit he felt he had achieved success and made progress, until the true meaning of the Tenth Commandment dawned on him. "Thou shalt not covet." He had not kept that, and with no amount of effort could he come anywhere near to keeping that! "I had not known lust," he wrote, "except the law had said, Thou shalt not covet" (Rom. VII.7). It was when he faced this Commandment and began to see that God demanded the whole obedience of the heart and of the desire as well as the whole obedience of the outward life, that he realised just how great a sinner he was. "Though he was able to prevent his evil desires from realising themselves in outward acts of hatred, or impurity or greed or slander, he was powerless to check, and still more powerless to destroy, the growing fount of lawless desire within him, or free himself from inward longings after the sins in which he refused to indulge outwardly" (R. H. Charles *The Decalogue*, p. 262).

It was when they were measured by God against the Tenth Commandment that the elder sons of Jesse failed hopelessly in His sight. Samuel was sent by God to Jesse's house to choose one of his sons as King of Israel. And the most likely of them were all presented first to Samuel for his judgment. They were all good upright boys, leaders of men, blameless in their outward behaviour, and of fine character, especially Eliab the elder of them all. "Surely the Lord's anointed is before Him," said Samuel to himself when he saw Eliab brought into the room to stand before him. But the Lord said to Samuel, "Look not on his countenance, or on the height of his stature; because I have refused him: for the Lord seeth not as man seeth; for man looketh on the outward appearance, but the Lord looketh on the heart" (1 Sam. XVI.7).

When we face the problem of the human heart we are also facing the whole problem of human sin and unhappiness at its deepest level. No one was more clear on this point in the Old Testament than the wise man who wrote the book of Proverbs: "Keep thy heart with all diligence; for out of it are the issues *as social activity ensu* ✗

of life" (Prov. iv.23). And in the New Testament it is James, the Lord's brother, who dwells on the same point in his Epistle. We are apt to imagine that if evil can dominate the environment it is inevitably bound to have the upperhand in the battle for the human soul. But James asserts that the strength of any temptation, arises not from what is outside us in the world around, but from what is already within us in our own inner desires. "Let no man say when he is tempted, I am tempted of God: for God cannot be tempted with evil, neither tempteth he any man: But every man is tempted when he is drawn away by his own lust, and enticed. And lust when it hath conceived bringeth forth sin, and sin when it is full grown, bringeth forth death" (Jas. 1.13–16). In writing all this he is simply echoing the teaching of Jesus Himself who said, "Whatsoever thing from without entereth into the man, it cannot defile him . . . that which cometh out of a man, that defileth the man" (Mk. vii.18, 20).

Source ?
Temptation

Time and again in the stories of the Bible we are shown that personal failure and tragedy is most often due to the weakness of the heart, often expressing itself first in the nursing and encouragement of some inward covetous desire. We can think of Achan, coveting the forbidden loot, and allowing his covetousness expression in an act of deceit that brought bitter consequences to all the people of his house. We can think of David first coveting the wife of Uriah the Hittite and then allowing his covetousness expression in sloth, treachery, and murder. We can think of Gehazi, of Ananias and Sapphira, of Judas. And the worst aspect of all those tragedies is that they were men who were otherwise outwardly good and noble.

But James pursues the argument even further. He insists that when we face the problem of the desires of the heart, we are facing the root of the whole problem of war and crime and social injustice . "From whence come wars and fightings among you? come they not hence, even of your lusts that war in your members? Ye lust, and have not: ye kill, and desire to have, and cannot obtain; ye fight and war, yet ye have not, because ye ask not" (Jas. iv.1–2). In saying this he is, again, repeating in his own way what he learned from Jesus and the Tenth Commandment.

✗

We sometimes express our concern over the amount of sordid human activity which we find thrust on our attention by some of our daily and Sunday newspapers. But Jesus, Himself, in the list He once made of the social evils of his day showed himself no less aware of the variety of the problem: "Evil thoughts, adulteries, fornications, murders, thefts, covetousness, wickedness, deceit, lasciviousness, an evil eye, blasphemy, pride, foolishness." What is more significant than the comprehensive nature of the catalogue, is the fact that after He made it, He repeated what He had already said before, "All these evil things come from within" (Mk. vii. 20–3).

But in spite of the fact that this is the root of the matter, the very problem of the covetous desire of the human heart is made more acute by the nature of the society in which we are born and brought up. It has been called "the acquisitive society." The fierce competition between man and man, firm and firm, group and group, which is the basis of its main driving power can only be kept going by the constant and fresh supply of a growing body of men and women who are geared into it by covetous desire and self-centred ambition. Their individual motive power must come from the desire to achieve the highest status and earn the maximum salary in the shortest possible time, the main non-material motive being the urgency of "keeping up with the Joneses" in style and outlook. At the same time, to create the demand for the products of this system we have to stimulate the desire to possess what it offers, and we do so by increasingly stimulating the appetite for possession, and increasingly complicating the basic human wants.

While much general good can come from the rising standards of living produced even in such a strange way, nevertheless in the midst of the whole process, the individual tends to become lost and his outlook warped. He becomes deprived of the will to resist the lawless tendencies of the heart which God seeks to call under control in this very Commandment. Self-expression becomes more important than self-control. Children from their earliest years are trained to imagine that nothing much matters but success in this game of pushing and grabbing, and that unless one fights ruthlessly in this battle to possess and succeed, one is bound to face failure and tragedy indeed. Far too often they are trained in the frank exercise of covetousness under the name of ambition. No one has put this better than Aldous Huxley: "Among the psychological elements which have been co-ordinated in the modern successful personality, the most important are the acquisitive tendencies. These have been moralised not by any process of sublimation but by a simple reversal of values. What was previously black is now called white. Covetousness, which was a deadly sin in the days of our medieval ancestors is now one of the cardinal virtues." A very widespread, striking, and sometimes even alarming, symptom of all this is the prevalence and increase of gambling. But the root cause of the disease should be more alarming to us than the symptom. Surely if we are going to condemn the gearing of covetousness into games of chance, we should even more forcibly condemn the gearing of covetousness into the basis of ordinary people's daily lives.

2. The heart of the cure

The Tenth Commandment is given not to make us despair, but to help us to know where to begin the reformation of our life under the promise of God. God does not take us to the heart of the problem without giving us hope that if we begin here, He also will begin with us, even in this problem.

The promise of His help is hidden even in the form of the commandment. "Thou shalt not covet" can and does mean "Thou shalt not need to covet." It is a promise that God Himself will provide for us in everything we think we lack. We will not need even to covet what is our earthly neighbour's, since we share so much of what belongs to our heavenly neighbour. It takes us to the heart of the answer given by God to the Apostle Paul, when he besought the Lord twice for the deliverance from the particular "thorn in the flesh" which he was bound to feel as his own peculiar privation in life, and under the burden of which he was bound to covet the freedom of other men. "My grace is sufficient for thee: for my strength is made perfect in weakness" (II Cor. XII.9). "I have learned," Paul can say later, "in whatsoever state I am, therewith to be content. I know both how to be abased, and I know how to abound: everywhere and in all things I am instructed both how to be full and how to be hungry, both to abound and to suffer need" (Phil. iv.11–12).

Is there not something very rich here that we have to discover? God has given us so much in Jesus Christ that we need no longer make comparisons between ourselves and others with regard to possessions or talents or privileges or sufferings. Paul was never weary of asserting this emphatically. "All things are yours; whether Paul, or Apollos, or Cephas, or the world, or life, or death, or things present, or things to come; all are yours; and ye are Christ's; and Christ is God's" (1 Cor. iii.22–3). "He that spared not his own Son, but delivered him up for us all, how shall he not with him also freely give us all things?" (Rom. viii.32). How can any of us who believe this promise, and have grasped anything of its reality, now look round from what it holds out to us, give way to the spirit of covetousness, or nurse gloom or bitterness or envy even for one moment?

But even with such promises we ourselves require to exercise sheer straightforward discipline at the heart of our desires and motives. In this Commandment God directs us to the place where the brake must be put on. We cannot by such discipline cure the heart or change what is within us. We cannot by self-control turn bitterness into sweetness. But the Commandment directs us to grapple with what is within us.

Restraint should begin more directly with the mind, than with the desire. All through the Bible the control of the mind over the will and feeling is stressed. It is the covetous thought, that is the father of the covetous desire. There are few unpremeditated crimes. As in the story of David and Bathsheba, it is the mind that feeds and fans the appetite till it becomes uncontrollable, and conscripts the whole will and action into its fulfilment. "Woe to them," says Micah, "that devise iniquity, and work evil upon their beds! when the morning is light, they practice it, because it is in the power of their hand. And they covet fields, and take them by violence; and houses, and take them away" (Mic. ii.1–2). Jesus, pleading with his disciples to be different from the heathen in their anxieties and desires, asked them to give God more of their minds. "Consider the lilies," He began, and from this point He raised their minds to the thought of their Heavenly Father's love, in order that they might be saved from seeking after "all these things" which the heathen seek after (Mt. vi.28–33).

But to cure the heart of its inevitable self-centredness and carelessness can be the work of God alone. It was to this sheer miracle of God's new creation that both Jeremiah and Ezekiel looked for, as they lifted up their eyes above the sad and bitter circumstance of the people to whom they spoke, and assured them of better things to come. "Behold, the days come, saith the Lord that I will make a new covenant with the house of Israel. . . . I will put my law in their inward parts, and write it in their hearts" (Jer. xxxi.33); "A new heart also will I give you, and a new spirit will I put within you: and I will take away the stony heart out of your flesh, and I will give you an heart of flesh" (Ezek. xxxvi.26).

And now, says Paul, we live within this new age, not of the letter, but of the spirit. He speaks of this miracle in terms of the "ministration of the spirit" which "gives life" (ii Cor. iii.6), in terms of the law of the spirit of life in Christ which make us "free from the law of sin and death" (Rom. viii.2). But he speaks even more clearly of Christ "dwelling" in the heart which he well knows to be the source of so much that is evil. It is "Christ in you" that is "the hope of glory" (Col. i.27). It is Christ dwelling in the heart by faith, that transforms the vision and outlook and fellowship of those who believe (Eph. iii.17) and enables them to say "no longer I" (Gal ii.20). All this is the fulfilment of the command and promise of our Lord, Himself. "Abide in me, and I in you. As the branch cannot bear fruit of itself, except it abide in the vine; no more can ye, except ye abide in me. I am the vine, ye are the branches: He that abideth in me, and I in him, the same bringeth forth much fruit: for without me ye can do nothing" (Jn. xv.4–5).